# Pharmacists Guide to Starting, Acquiring or Selling a Pharmacy

## (Canadian Version)

## by Phil Hauser, CBB

My desire in writing this book is to educate both young pharmacy professionals looking to own a pharmacy for the first time, as well as the established owners group who wish to expand and make further acquisitions.

We will look at many essential steps that need to be taken to move towards a successful acquisition, start-up or ownership transition.

 **FriesenPress**

Suite 300 – 990 Fort Street
Victoria, BC, Canada V8V 3K2
www.friesenpress.com

**ISBN**
978-1-4602-5792-0 (Hardcover)
978-1-4602-5793-7 (Paperback)
978-1-4602-5794-4 (eBook)

*1. Medical, Pharmacy*

Distributed to the trade by The Ingram Book Company

# TABLE OF CONTENTS

# ACKNOWLEDGEMENTS

Special acknowledgement to my many friends,
colleagues and clients who encouraged and sup-
ported me in the writing of this book:


"Navin, Derek, Rod, Tim, John, Mike, Guy, Don, Riaz"
and the CFIB (Canadian Federation of Independent Business),


as well as my family and in particular my wife
Cheryl for her loving support in all things.


Phil Hauser

# FOREWORD

Many pharmacists today become enamoured with a vision of owning their own pharmacy. This is a very laudable goal, no doubt, but one that comes with many considerations that are often overlooked. By nature, pharmacists tend to be scientifically minded individuals who may not have a solid grasp of business concepts related to owning a business. The lack of intricate knowledge required for buying and selling a pharmacy business is further compounded by the fact that most pharmacy programs at Canadian universities do not have a strong business aspect to their curricula. As a result, graduating pharmacists are left to learn about business in general, and buying or selling a pharmacy in particular, through trial and error. This can be a very expensive way to get a business education.

While one could argue that the buying and selling of any small business is the same process regardless of the industry, I believe there are some unique aspects to the pharmacy business that make this book a must have resource. Pharmacy is both a business and a profession and sometimes those two aspects aren't in concert with one another. That is why the buying or selling of a pharmacy isn't as simple as it might be for a straight forward retail business. Phil Hauser has addressed many of those issues that are unique to the business and practice of pharmacy as they relate to buying or selling a business.

In this book, Phil has addressed all of the major important considerations when buying or selling an existing pharmacy or starting a new pharmacy from the ground up. This book provides practical guidance and key information for potential buyers and sellers of pharmacies. Furthermore, Phil has laid out all of the critical foundational knowledge required to make informed decisions about how to conduct the sale or purchase of your business. Even if you are not currently contemplating the sale or purchase of a pharmacy you may find some sections of this book extremely useful in helping you manage your current business. You'll gain a better understanding of the value of a business plan and the importance of engaging key professionals such as accountants and lawyers.

Some sections of the book are directed more at sellers than buyers, and vice versa, but it's strongly recommended that you read all sections because you'll find useful information from both perspectives in all sections. For example, while chapter 7 is mainly directed at sellers it would be important for you as a buyer to know how a seller is positioning their business. Conversely in Chapter 8, which is mainly directed at buyers, it will be highly useful for a seller to understand how a buyer views a possible acquisition and what they are looking for.

I wish you success in what might be one of the most challenging undertakings of your business career. I am very pleased to be able to recommend this book and the support services of Phil Hauser and White Heart Lane Consulting Ltd. as excellent resources that I am sure will help you achieve your goals. Finally, I encourage you to register on Phil's website at www.rxownership.ca so that you can access all of the great resources that are available there to supplement the detailed information in this book.

**Derek Desrosiers**
**President**
**Desson Consulting Ltd.**
*(www.dessonconsulting.com)*

# INTRODUCTION

I am a soccer nut! While writing this book the World Cup in Brazil has come to conclusion with Germany winning its fourth World Cup. Needless to say – being a fan of the "Deutscher Fussbal-Bund" – I was very pleased with the result. After the tournament was over I read the background on how Germany prepared for the tournament. I was surprised at the years of preparation and intense planning and finally the execution of a process that brought about this milestone in German football. This outcome for Germany was years in the making requiring extensive planning, thinking and strategy to get the result that I'm sure seemed far off and difficult at times to achieve.

The desire to acquire, start-up or even sell a pharmacy is not un-similar although quite different. In many ways, for a pharmacy professional getting into ownership either through start-up or acquisition, they can be faced with a lot of competition. Sometimes, as in Germany's case, it can be years in the making. Everyone is different with their individual pace, style and work ethic. What is constant and what I try to address in this book is the preparation, planning and process necessary to realize the outcome that seems far off and difficult to achieve whether you're looking to acquire, start-up or perhaps even sell a pharmacy.

The independent pharmacy landscape is changing rapidly. How pharmacy is reimbursed and the product and professional services offered is changing as the scope of pharmacy practise evolves to become more essential and integrated with the healthcare system. Change is in the air as pharmacy owners try to adapt and manage. In the midst of all this we are faced with a demographic reality. The reality is an aging population of business owners in Canada. In addition to succession of independent pharmacy ownership, I have found that many pharmacy professionals who wish to get into ownership for the first time are seriously unprepared. This book endeavours to discuss both the dynamics in the marketplace in terms of an aging population of pharmacy owners as well as what a pharmacy professional needs to consider moving forward towards their ownership goals.

This aging population of owners also includes independent pharmacy. In a research paper on succession (2011) from the Canadian Federation of Independent Business (CFIB), the results showed that ownership transition will be approximately 75% over the next 10 years. It also revealed that about 80% of the business owners had no succession plan and that only 10% had an idea of what succession might look like for them individually. Stats Canada (2008) states that in the healthcare sector, 89% of the enterprises are small to medium. This statistic would include pharmacy, dental practises, chiropractic, etc. The CFIB goes on to report that the majority of owners that plan on exiting their businesses in the next five years are typically those who have been in business for a least 11 years and those aged 50 and over. This report also goes on to list several key barriers to succession planning. I think it is important to list the top five reasons here.

# BARRIERS TO SUCCESSION PLANNING

1. Finding a suitable buyer;

2. Valuing the business;

3. Financing for the buyer;

4. Too much dependence on the owner's involvement post-closing; and

5. Access to cost effective professional advice.

It has become very evident to me that the independent pharmacy sector needs to have access to effective and comprehensive professional advice. As a result, I launched Rxownership.ca to assist first time buyers or younger pharmacy professionals as well as the established owners group looking to create an effective succession plan for the best possible outcome.

There is a real danger that without proper succession planning and without qualified buyers to take over these pharmacy businesses, the results could be catastrophic to the Canadian economy, needless to say the impact on independent pharmacy and the healthcare system.

In my role as an independent pharmacy succession and acquisitions consultant for almost 10 years, I am amazed at how many pharmacy professionals are interested in owning and operating an independent pharmacy for the first time. The majority of the pharmacy professionals that I come into contact with are younger and are working in an independent pharmacy, a corporately owned pharmacy or hospital pharmacy. Some are staff pharmacists and others are pharmacy managers with a different level of experience and responsibility. This group tends to have a "romantic" view of ownership without a clear understanding of what it takes to acquire a pharmacy or to start one from scratch. Another group actively looking for further ownership are the established owners group. This group consists of current pharmacy owners, either solely or in partnership, looking to expand their ownership portfolios by adding further acquisitions.

What I have discovered is that in regards to the younger pharmacy professionals as well as the established owners group, is that the majority of them do not know how to acquire a pharmacy and what I call the *preparation, planning and process* of pharmacy ownership. As a result of this lack of understanding, many acquisitions are never achieved.

It's not just a lack of understanding that keeps both the younger pharmacy professionals and the established owners group from successfully making acquisitions, it's also their major competition. This competition consists of corporate acquisitions teams for large corporate entities in the Canadian market who are aggressive and actively pursuing acquisitions. These strategic buyers are knowledgeable and systematic in regards to acquisitions, and as a result they tend to be more successful. Some might argue that the success of the strategic buyers is a result of larger budgets than the younger pharmacy professionals looking to own for the first time, or the established owners group. However, from my experience in dealings with all of these groups, I find that this is not always the case. In my additional role as a succession consultant for independent pharmacy owners, one might generally assume that "it's all about the money". My experience differs in that I find that during my succession consults, I find more often that it is a combination of legacy and money that satisfies many pharmacy owners.

In addition to making an acquisition, I am consistently asked what the difference is in making an acquisition of an independent pharmacy, verses starting an independent pharmacy from scratch, or as it is commonly referred to in the industry as a "Greenfield start-up." In many ways, both potential business ventures differ, while in some respects they are quite similar. In some ways the risks are similar, and in many ways the business plan applications differ.

My desire in writing this book is to educate both young pharmacy professionals looking to own a pharmacy for the first time, as well as the established owners group who wish to expand and make further acquisitions. We will look at many essential steps that need to be taken to move towards a successful acquisition or start-up.

# CHAPTER ONE –
# THE BUSINESS PLAN

In the hundreds of conversations that I have had with younger pharmacy professionals over the last 10 years who wish to acquire or start-up a pharmacy, I could only count on one hand the number who had attempted to write a business plan. In addition, the same number would apply to the established owners group in terms of a written plan. It runs correspondently with the number of pharmacy owners who have a written succession plan.

So why is a written business plan so important? I have had two opportunities in the last 12 months to speak to 4th year students in the Pharmacy Faculty of a major Canadian university on this subject, and we need to understand that independent pharmacy is a somewhat unique business. How independent pharmacies get reimbursed now, and how they will be reimbursed in the future is changing. How business plans are written should be adapting as well. In the pharmacy industry we tend to think that most people understand how pharmacy works, but that is not the case. As an example, 10 years ago no one knew what a "generic drug rebate" was, and if you did know, you kept that information to yourself.

Unless they currently have a number of independent pharmacy clients, bankers and other financial institutions, lawyers, and accounting professionals don't have a complete understanding of the challenges, operations, valuation and reimbursement of an independent pharmacy. Writing a business plan will help those you wish to share it with to grasp what your professional practise, in the context of independent ownership, will look like.

Writing a business plan is equally important in making a pharmacy acquisition or doing a start-up. Whether you are a younger pharmacy professional, or if you belong to the established owners group, writing a business plan is where you should begin your preparation.

First, other than the aforementioned reasons for writing a business plan, I would like to tell you about an independent pharmacy owner I know. For the interests of anonymity, I'll call him Micky. When I got to know Micky, he already owned several pharmacies and I was engaged to assist him in acquiring the next one. The first thing Micky did when he prepared to acquire a pharmacy was . . . yes, you guessed it, he wrote a business plan. By assisting Micky with this acquisition I learned that without fail he always wrote a business plan first of all, because of the impact it had on his preparation success.

In the case of his next acquisition, when he presented his business plan to his banker, not only did his banker get a clearer picture of what his professional practise model looked like, but his banker also shaved a one-half percent point off his business loan rate.

Some pharmacy professionals I have spoken to regard writing a business plan as a project rather than as a blueprint for success. For those successful independent pharmacy owners out there like Micky, the business plan is considered a blueprint. I call it a working document because it can be added to or components can be deleted or adjusted as you move forward. Writing a business plan for an independent pharmacy acquisition or a pharmacy start-up should not be a large document.

Most of the ones I have seen or helped with are approximately 10 pages (to start).

Writing a business plan can have a profound effect on a partnership in terms of its success and longevity. I will speak more about partnerships later on in this book. You may be thinking – why write a business plan for an acquisition, when there should be one in place already. I have yet to see an independent pharmacy owner who has been in business for many years to actually have a written plan. That does not mean there is no plan, and if you sit with them long enough and ask the right questions, you will find out what the business plan looks like. It becomes an oral history, rather than a written history of why the pharmacy in question has been successful so far.

So if you were interested in acquiring a pharmacy with no written business plan (and there is a high percentage out there), why and how would your written business plan matter? I will share the story of a couple looking to make their first pharmacy acquisition. We'll call them Diane and Denis.

When I met them, I was representing the owner of an established and successful pharmacy. The owner had been in business at the current location for many years and was set to retire. I was able to consult Diane and Denis on the preparation, planning and process of making a pharmacy acquisition, and the short story is that they became the new owners of this pharmacy. As part of the pre-closing negotiations and discussion during a due diligence meeting that I hosted, was that the current owner would stay on and work in the pharmacy part-time as part of the ownership transition (a good plan).

About six months into their new tenure as owners, I received a call from them advising they were quite anxious that the business performance was off and the numbers were starting to reflect it. I immediately asked what had changed in their mind, from when they were first introduced to the existing business plan (orally). She went on to explain that they had introduced their business plan almost immediately when they took over, and could not understand why the business was stuttering. A couple of days later I received a call from the previous owner who was now working part-time. He was quite anxious as well, and explained how business was dropping off, and that the new owners' business plan was not working. I told him I would speak to them. I called one of the new owners and said that I had spoken to the previous owner and he had expressed his concerns. I asked both the new owners to meet with the previous owner and discuss their new business plan in detail against the proven successes of the old one.

The end result was that the business got back on track and business moved forward as planned. What I learned from this example is that a new business plan must not be brought in and smother the old one or sweep the old one away and replace it. Both plans must merge and become *one business plan* and continue to evolve as the pharmacy business and pharmacy practise changes over time.

Even though there may very well be components of the old business plan that are not working, there will be essential components that are, and for the immediate future they will make up a solid foundation for the pharmacy business. I firmly believe that any new business plan brought into an acquisition must, over time, dovetail or weave into the old one for the business to thrive and move forward. After all, after paying significant money for a pharmacy business and good will in particular, it only makes sense to work through the business plan merger as well. Below is what I call key components to a pharmacy business plan (not in any particular order). A properly drafted plan should not be limited to these points, however, they represent essentials.

Key components to a business plan:

- Operating Company (Opco);

- Competitive Analysis;

- Demographic Analysis;

- Proximity to Doctors;

- SWOT Analysis;

- Pro forma;

- Financing; and

- Eventual Succession.

# PRO FORMA

Pro forma is a Latin term meaning "for the sake of form". In the business world it describes a method of calculating financial results in order to draw attention to *current achievements* or to *project future performance*. A Pro forma should be included with any independent pharmacy business plan. In the case of an acquisition, a Pro forma should be based on the current performance of the potential acquisition as expressed in the financial statements made available to a potential buyer.

The Pro forma should provide you with key performance indicators which will project a "rate of return" (ROR) on your investment and calculate a payback waypoint or "return on investment" (ROI). A Pro forma statement is set up similar to an income statement (or P&L, statement of earnings, etc.). It is designed to look forward towards the future performance of the pharmacy business in the case of an acquisition, based on historical performance.

The Pro forma should also indicate performance indicators as a result of changes in the business plan. If for instance, as an owner you believe there will be less revenue generated from a product or service offering or perhaps more revenue generated over a specific period of time, the Pro forma should indicate the projected change. The same holds true for expenses and whether or not there will be changes in the historical amount of expenses incurred.

This information is critical in the decision making process of the pharmacy business owner, or owners, as well as the directors of the company. The Pro forma also assists the individuals with whom you might share the business plan with, i.e. bankers, potential partners, etc. In terms of a start-up pharmacy (or Greenfield), the Pro forma will define how the pharmacy business will begin to generate revenue as well as the anticipated expenses. This information defined by the Pro forma and included in the business plan will be helpful when seeking financing.

One key indicator for a start-up pharmacy is "cash burn". Cash burn is a defined as *a measure for how fast a company will use up its shareholder capital before the breakeven point*. Remember you will need enough cash in the bank to pay your expenses and yourself, staff etc., until you reach that breakeven point. Your lender is going to want to know, based on your business plan, when that might be. Proving that you can create a Pro forma is an indicator of your financial aptitude.

Demonstrating that you understand how sales flow through the various financial statements and the impact that your spending decisions can have on cash flow and profitability show the intended reader that you have an understanding of the business of running a pharmacy. Another benefit to writing a Pro forma is that it gives you a framework under which you can test your assumptions.

A good Pro forma will allow you to examine different scenarios that may present themselves as you start your pharmacy business. Believe it or not, more sales are not always the answer to more profit. Your Pro forma can help you predict what the desired mix of sales and expenses should be to grow your pharmacy business. At the end of the day, the most important reason for creating your Pro forma is to help you understand whether your entrepreneurial endeavour will be worth your while.

This is a big help in getting past the "'romantic" view of owning a pharmacy business and looking at the business end realistically and at face value. When your start-up, financial assumptions have been properly presented and tested within the Pro forma and you can often get a more objective view of the market value of your idea. Not every start-up is a good idea and not every good idea is a profitable one.

So take the time to create the Pro forma and share it with as many advisors as will honestly review the document. *It will likely save you time and money.* Below are four steps to getting started on a Pro forma. Don't forget to ask a trusted advisor for help and input. I would also suggest asking a current pharmacy owner (if you know one) what components should be considered as well.

## STEP 1

Calculate revenue projections for the business. You must use realistic market assumptions in order to write a well-balanced and accurate Pro forma. Look through trade publications and speak to people inside the pharmacy industry, such as individuals at your provincial Pharmacy Association, to determine what a normal annual revenue stream for the industry is. This includes cash flow, fixtures, leasehold improvements, computers, etc. and what normal "net book value" (NBV) looks like for a pharmacy.

## STEP 2

Estimate your liabilities and expenses. Your liabilities will be such things as business loans and lines of credit. Your expenses will be your lease, payroll, insurance, licenses, permits, inventory and operating expenses like utilities. Revenue projections from Step 1 and cost projections from this step will make up the first part of the Pro forma.

## STEP 3

Estimate cash flows. These comprise projected future revenue, future purchases and sales of business assets (i.e. inventory and professional services), as well as the future issuance of dividend payouts (if applicable). Demonstrating cash flows is the second portion of a Pro forma.

# STEP 4

Create a spreadsheet (and charts if you can) that will present the Pro forma over a three to five year period. The first year's projections of profits and expenses should be broken down in monthly increments. The second and third year's projections should be divided quarterly. For the fourth and fifth year, the projections should be annual.

Pro-Forma Income Statement

My Pharmacy Ltd
(all numbers in $000)

| | 2012 | 2013 | 2014 | 2015 |
|---|---|---|---|---|
| **REVENUE** | | | | |
| Gross sales | $500 | $650 | $720 | $850 |
|    Less sales returns and allowances | 200 | 230 | 280 | 320 |
| Net Sales | $300 | $420 | $440 | $530 |
| | | | | |
| **COST OF SALES** | | | | |
| Beginning inventory | $350 | $360 | $420 | $435 |
|    Plus goods purchased / manufactured | 120 | 165 | 185 | 190 |
| Total Goods Available | $470 | $525 | $605 | $625 |
|    Less ending inventory | 360 | 420 | 435 | 440 |
| Total Cost of Goods Sold | $110 | $105 | $170 | $185 |
| | | | | |
| Gross Profit (Loss) | $190 | $315 | $270 | $345 |
| | | | | |
| **OPERATING EXPENSES** | | | | |
| Selling | | | | |
|    Salaries and wages | $35 | $41 | $46 | $52 |
|    Commissions | 12 | 14 | 16 | 18 |
|    Advertising | 10 | 12 | 14 | 20 |
|    Depreciation | 14 | 15 | 16 | 16 |
|    Other | 5 | 6 | 6 | 7 |
| Total Selling Expenses | $76 | $88 | $98 | $113 |
| | | | | |
| General/Administrative | | | | |
|    Salaries and wages | $12 | $14 | $16 | $18 |
|    Employee benefits | 4 | 5 | 5 | 6 |
|    Payroll taxes | 2 | 3 | 3 | 4 |
|    Insurance | 6 | 6 | 7 | 7 |
|    Rent | 8 | 8 | 9 | 9 |
|    Utilities | 2 | 2 | 2 | 3 |
|    Depreciation & amortization | 3 | 4 | 4 | 5 |
|    Office supplies | 1 | 1 | 1 | 1 |
|    Travel & entertainment | 3 | 3 | 3 | 4 |
|    Postage | 1 | 1 | 1 | 2 |
|    Equipment maintenance & rental | 0 | 0 | 1 | 1 |
|    Interest | 0 | 1 | 1 | 2 |
|    Furniture & equipment | 3 | 4 | 4 | 5 |
| Total General/Administrative Expenses | $45 | $52 | $57 | $67 |
| | | | | |
| Total Operating Expenses | $121 | $140 | $155 | $180 |
| | | | | |
| | | | | |
| Net Income Before Taxes | $69 | $175 | $115 | $165 |
|    Taxes on income | 22 | 32 | 26 | 28 |
| Net Income After Taxes | $47 | $143 | $89 | $137 |
| | | | | |
| Extraordinary gain or loss | $0 | $0 | $43 | $0 |
| Income tax on extraordinary gain | 0 | 0 | 12 | 0 |
| | | | | |
| **NET INCOME (LOSS)** | $47 | $143 | $120 | $137 |

## OPERATING COMPANY (OPCO)

Establishing an operating company is an important step in a pharmacy business plan, whether you are looking for an acquisition or contemplating a pharmacy start-up. In my many years of consulting independent pharmacy owners, I have only come across one or two who have operated as "sole proprietors". Let's look at some of the basic differences between a sole proprietorship and a corporation.

# STARTING A COMPANY

## SOLE PROPRIETOR

With this type of business organization, you would be fully responsible for all debts and obligations related to your business and all profits would be yours alone to keep. As a sole owner of the business, a creditor can make a claim against your personal or business assets to pay off any debt. A sole proprietorship is one person operating a business, without forming a corporation. The income of the business is then taxed as the owner (the proprietor), at personal income tax rates. The income is considered income from self-employment, and is included on the personal income tax return of the owner.

For income tax purposes, as a self-employed sole proprietorship, the proprietor must report all business income including any living and travel allowance received. Reasonable expenses can be deducted from the business income, including travel expenses, depreciation of an automobile, legal, accounting/ bookkeeping, insurance, etc. I would advise speaking to an accounting professional to clearly understand the tax implications of a proprietorship.

## ADVANTAGES OF SOLE PROPRIETORSHIP

Setting up a business as a sole proprietorship is relatively simple and the costs are reasonable. If the business loses money, the losses can be written off against other income of the proprietor.

Sole proprietorships are less regulated than corporations. The administration is less costly than that of a corporation. That being said, sole proprietorships are regulated by the provincial/territorial governments, and the sole proprietorship may have to be registered. The proprietor is in control of all decision making and receives all profits of the business.

## DISADVANTAGES OF SOLE PROPRIETORSHIP

The most significant disadvantage of a sole proprietorship is unlimited liability. The proprietor is liable for all debts and other liabilities of the business. If the business is sued, all the business and personal assets of the owner are at risk.

If the business is profitable, it will usually be paying higher taxes than if it wasn't. The lowest personal income tax rate paid by a sole proprietorship would range from approximately 20% to 29%, depending on the province/territory. This rate increases with income. A sole proprietorship is not as permanent as a corporation – if the owner dies, the net business assets pass to the heirs, but valuable leases and contracts may not. It would be advisable to discuss a sole proprietorship with your lawyer before deciding if it is the best course for your business plan.

# INCORPORATION

Another type of business structure is incorporation. Incorporation can be done at the federal or provincial/territorial level. When you incorporate your business, it is considered to be a legal entity that is separate from the owners and shareholders. As a shareholder of a corporation, you will not be personally liable for the debts, obligations or acts of the corporation. When making a decision to incorporate, it is always wise to seek legal advice before incorporating.

## ADVANTAGES OF INCORPORATION

- Limited liability;

- Ownership is transferable;

- Continuous existence;

- Separate legal entity;

- Easier to raise capital; and

- Possible tax advantage as taxes may be lower for an incorporated business.

## DISADVANTAGES

- A corporation is closely regulated;

- More expensive to incorporate than a partnership or sole proprietorship;

- Extensive corporate records are required, including shareholder and director meetings, and documentation filed annually with the government;

- Possible conflict between shareholders and directors; and

- Possible problems with residency of directors.

In addition to informing potential customers about your pharmacy if you're choosing a start-up, you must let the government know about your plans. You may need to register with several different levels of government for various reasons.

# WHAT TO CONSIDER IN CHOOSING A NAME

The right name can be an effective advertising tool that can help your customers understand what your pharmacy does and which market you are targeting. The wrong name can confuse or drive away customers.

# SOME THINGS TO THINK ABOUT

**Does it describe the product or service you offer?**

You don't want to waste your customers' time or give them the wrong impression about your products or professional services, especially when you can't always control the impression in which they first see or hear about your business.

**Does it reflect the values of your business plan?**

Think about how you want your business to be perceived.

**Is the name distinctive?**

It is important to differentiate yourself from the competition and allow customers to identify you as a unique brand. Choose a name that doesn't already exist in the market. Unless you plan to have a fairly aggressive marketing strategy, keep your name simple and avoid abbreviations.

**Can customers identify and remember it?**

Names that are easy to pronounce and spell will help customers remember you. It may be fun to choose a name that has personal significance, but see the name through your target market's eyes.

**Are you legally allowed to use it?**

By law, the name of your business can't be the same as (or very similar to) an existing corporate name or trade-mark. You will want to do an online name search once you have an idea for a name to be sure that it is unique. You can also have your attorney perform a search to see if the name you have chosen is available.

Your Business Number is a nine-digit account number that identifies your business to federal and provincial governments. You can open several different accounts for your business through a single registration. The accounts include:

- GST/HST;

- Payroll deductions;

- Corporate income tax;

- Import/export; and

- Other federal and provincial accounts.

In order to do business in Canada, and to comply with government regulations, you will need a licence to practise pharmacy and permits from different levels of government. Please take time to contact your provincial College of Pharmacy for details on the application, process and requirements.

# EVENTUAL SUCCESSION

Every independent pharmacy business plan should include a succession component. Succession is not always defined as retirement. Succession from ownership can include lifestyle changes as well as partnership. Succession in my experience always starts with the desired outcome. What does the succession plan outcome look like and when will it take place? I have known many successful independent pharmacy owners who have built a successful business model to a point where the model peaks. As a result they sell the pharmacy business and look to build on their business plan and apply the new model at a new location where they see the most opportunity to succeed. Some very entrepreneurial independent pharmacy owners I know have done this multiple times.

I will discuss partnerships later on in this book and the impact of partnerships on the pharmacy business and business plan.

# CHAPTER TWO – CAST OF SUPPORTING PROFESSIONALS

## MERGERS AND ACQUISITIONS CONSULTANT

In my experience as an M&A Consultant for independent pharmacy professionals, the efforts of the M&A Consultant, in many cases, will assist the pharmacy professional with sound advice on either an acquisition or start-up. This is because the interests of the M&A Consultant are in sync with the goals of the pharmacy professional. You need to know what the current market activity is, and as a result, what steps need to be taken to ensure you have begun to prepare for independent pharmacy ownership. In other words, a pharmacy professional that uses an M&A advisor can end up with a far better ownership outcome than a pharmacy professional that does not.

Starting or acquiring a pharmacy business is a skill in and of itself which is different from the skill of running a business. Even though most pharmacy professionals are highly skilled at running their businesses, they are not necessarily skilled at starting or acquiring a pharmacy business. These are two entirely different processes and attempting to acquire or start-up a pharmacy business without fully understanding how to do it can have serious negative consequences and end up costing more than anticipated. I know of numerous pharmacy professionals who have tried to acquire or start-up pharmacies on their own and have ended up making serious mistakes primarily because they don't know what is "normal" in an acquisition or start-up of a pharmacy business. An M&A advisor works on numerous transactions and knows what acquisition or start-up terms are reasonable and what are unreasonable. This expertise can save a pharmacy professional tens of thousands of dollars.

# LAWYER (MERGERS & ACQUISITIONS) ATTORNEY

**Not all lawyers specialize in mergers and acquisitions.** As you know lawyers specialize in numerous disciplines including family law, insurance, corporate law, etc. It is important to know an M&A lawyer as a resource for building and executing a business plan. M&A attorneys deal with the selling and buying of businesses. In recent years, the number of overall mergers and acquisitions has increased and will continue as an aging population of owners' transition out of ownership. M&A attorneys are involved with everything from small start-up companies to giant corporations. Whether you are acquiring a pharmacy or engaging in a start-up, here are a few tips to help you choose the right M&A attorney.

## SHOP AROUND
Do your homework to find a solid M&A attorney with experience and pharmacy industry knowledge. Ask for references from pharmacy associates and other attorneys whom you know of.

## KNOW THE FEES

While some attorneys may charge an hourly rate, others may charge a flat fee for all legal services. Before you sign an engagement letter or agree to a retainer, make sure any prospective attorney clearly explains how you will be charged and an estimate of how much you can expect to pay in total. However, don't let cost alone become your sole deciding factor. When it comes to attorneys, you get what you pay for, and experienced, more qualified lawyers are simply going to cost more.

## INQUIRE ABOUT EXPERIENCE

Ask potential attorneys how much experience they have in mergers and acquisitions, and specifically how many transactions they typically complete in a year. Be sure to ask if they have experience handling pharmacy ownership goals similar to yours.

## CONTACT THE LOCAL BAR ASSOCIATION

Most provincial bars can provide a list of highly qualified, experienced attorneys in your area who specialize specifically in M&A.

## ASK QUESTIONS

Consider compiling a list of questions to discuss with your potential M&A attorney during initial consultations. You should consider asking for an approximate timeframe of how long typical acquisitions take and whether or not you should be looking to purchase shares or assets. Also include more general questions like whether or not junior attorneys or paralegals in the firm will share the caseload and how you will be contacted when there are developments (i.e. face-to-face meetings, emails, phone calls, etc.). Having an experienced M&A attorney can make all the difference in a cost effective and comprehensive outcome for your pharmacy acquisition or start-up.

I would like to share a story that I heard from a fellow M&A consultant who told me about a deal between a pharmacy owner and a prospective buyer several years ago. In this case, the M&A consultant had done all of his preparation and consulting to help ensure a succession plan was in place with the seller, as well as make sure everything was in order to engage a potential buyer.

Once a qualified buyer was engaged and the letter of intent was signed, due diligence was completed. The M&A consultant working on this deal went on to explain that the seller chose a large firm based on their experienced team of qualified legal professionals. The seller did not however, have a clear picture on what the fees for this legal transaction were going to look like. The buyer on the other hand had chosen the least expensive lawyer he could find.

What happened next was that the lawyer for the buyer, realizing he was in over his head, farmed out the lion's share of the work to a larger firm (without the knowledge of the buyer) to try and get the deal done and in effect, ramping up the legal costs. The conclusion of this story is that the proposed deal fell through due to frustration on behalf of the seller and the buyer with their respective legal representatives and other related issues. Both the seller and the buyer ended up paying legal fees beyond their expectations for a deal that never happened.

Granted there is more to this story than I am able to share here, and the seller and the buyer had the responsibility to perform further due diligence regarding their respective legal representatives, however, the point is to take the steps and be sure you have the right M&A attorney with a fee structure you are comfortable with before you begin to execute your plan.

# CHAPTER THREE – FINANCING YOUR PHARMACY BUSINESS

In numerous conversations I have had with colleagues who represent companies that finance pharmacies, I have gleaned the following as essential when looking at financing options. I would recommend meeting with various lenders and sharing your business plan with them to determine the best financing option(s) for you. Whether you are planning on starting a pharmacy or making an acquisition, more than likely you will need some form of capital, which simply refers to the money that finances your business.

One reason for the failure of many small businesses is that they undercapitalize their business. Therefore, it is important that you know how much money you will actually need to start and to run your business until you reach your break-even point— the point when your sales revenue equals your total expenses.

## ASK YOURSELF THESE BASIC QUESTIONS

- How much money is required to start this pharmacy business?

- How much of your own money do you have for this pharmacy business?

- Do you already own any of the assets needed to start this pharmacy business?

- Do you have family, friends, acquaintances, or potential partners who are willing and able to invest in this pharmacy business?

- Do you have a strong personal credit rating or lines of credit available?

## EQUITY INVESTMENT

Equity means ownership. With equity investment, an investor makes money available for use in exchange for an ownership share in the pharmacy business. If you use equity investment, be sure to consider how much ownership you are willing to give up, and at what price. Once you sell 51% of your shares, you lose control of your company.

Equity investment includes any money from individuals, including yourself or other companies in your pharmacy business. This money may be from personal savings, inheritance, personal loans, friends or relatives, partners, or other shareholders. These funds are not secured on any of your business assets.

But before going down this road, it is important to know the provincial laws that apply to any company or other entity that raises money from investors.

# PERSONAL SAVINGS: THE MOST COMMON FORM OF EQUITY INVESTMENT

You will likely get most of your start-up funding from your personal savings, inheritances, friends, or family. For instance, according to Statistics Canada's Survey of Financing of Small and Medium Enterprises 2007, 76% of small businesses in British Columbia financed their business with personal savings.

Consider funding 25% to 50% of your business from your own pocket. This shows other prospective lenders and investors that you are personally assuming some risk, and are committed to your pharmacy's success. It is also a requirement for many small business loans which are usually secured or "backed by assets".

Throughout the course of your pharmacy's business, try to keep a personal investment of at least 25% in your business to increase your equity position and leverage. The more equity your business has, the more attractive it makes you to banks that can loan you up to three times your equity.

# DEBT FINANCING

## GOVERNMENT FUNDING

Typically the most sought-after type of financing is government grants because it is free money that you do not have to pay back. Unfortunately, a grant might not be an option for your business because not only are there very few grants available, most are geared towards specific industries or groups of people such as youth, women, or aboriginal owners.

The majority of government funding programs are typically loans which you will be required to repay the principal amount plus interest.

In 2007, only 2% of businesses obtained some sort of government funding or assistance. You can find information about government funding programs for free.

- Search the Canada Business Grants and Finances section, which lists available government programs across Canada.

- Contact your provincial pharmacy association to find out if they know of any grants you might be eligible to receive.

Since the application process varies from program to program, you should contact the coordinator of the program that you are interested in to find out what the specific application requirements and process are.

## COMMERCIAL LOANS

Commercial or personal loans from financial institutions account for the second most common form of financing at 44%.

- Long-term loans: Use long-term loans for larger expenses or for fixed assets that you expect to use for more than one year, such as property, buildings, vehicles, and equipment. These loans are generally secured by new assets, other physical business assets, and/or additional stakeholder funds or personal guarantees.

- Short-term loans: Short-term loans are usually for a one-year term or less and can include revolving lines of credit or credit cards. These are generally used to finance day-to-day expenses such as inventory, payroll, and unexpected or emergency items, and can be subject to a higher base interest rate.

## GETTING YOUR LOAN APPROVED: WHAT DO POTENTIAL LENDERS LOOK FOR?

Many lenders will look for the "four C's of Lending" when looking to approve a loan application:

1. **Cash flow** – Your ability to repay the cash you are borrowing. This is measured using the cash flow forecast that you created as part your business plan (Pro forma).

2. **Collateral** – The value of assets that you are willing to commit for assurance that you will repay your loan. A dollar amount will be placed on these assets and that will be compared to the amount of the loan you requested.

3. **Commitment** – The amount of money you are committing to your business. You cannot expect to qualify for a loan without contributing some funds yourself.

4. **Character** – Your personal credit score and history with the financial institution. Your credit rating or score is calculated from your history of borrowing and repaying bank loans, credit cards, and personal lines of credit. Without a good credit rating, your loan prospects decrease significantly.

A potential lender might determine how much to lend you by evaluating your cash flow, collateral, and commitment. They will then subtract your existing debt to arrive at a final amount. Note that lenders look at the limit on your credit cards as well, not the amount you are currently using.

Pharmacy start-ups are not rich in assets so you may be required to secure your business loans with personal collateral such as your house or vehicle(s).

Try to make a good impression with your lenders. You can increase your chances of securing a loan by:

- Having a properly written business plan/Pro forma;

- Having strong management and staff;

- Offering collateral;

- Having a strong personal credit rating;

- Always making your loan and interest payments on time, and never missing a payment.

In terms of making an acquisition the same principles described above apply. The difference in approaching financing is that there is historical data available which a potential lender can view and assess to determine value, level of risk and your ability to repay. In addition, the current performance/cash flow and assets of the acquisition in question come into play as well in terms of financing.

Mike Jaczko is a colleague of mine with a wealth of experience in independent pharmacy. Mike is currently a partner in KJ Harrison & Partners Inc. in Toronto, Ontario. (www.kjharrison.com). The following is a quick synopsis from Mike on the six key points of credit and six points on relationships.

## SIX KEY ELEMENTS OF CREDIT

- Character (integrity, preparedness, experience, communication);

- Capacity (sufficient cash flow to service debt obligations);

- Capital (net worth);

- Collateral (assets to ideally secure the debt);

- Financial companies have comfort in goodwill security;

- Conditions (of the borrower & the overall economy).

## RELATIONSHIPS WITH FINANCIAL INSTITUTIONS:

1. Financial institutions like relationships that:

   a. Provide comfort;

   b. Informative;

   c. Consultative and communicative.

2. Financial institutions expect preparation:

   a. Evidenced by financial statements and Pro formas;

b. Evidenced by a business plan.

3. Financial Institutions do not like surprises.

The following is a sample of a basic debt service payment Pro forma for an independent pharmacy:

# Example debt servicing schedule

| | | | | | | | | | |
|---|---|---|---|---|---|---|---|---|---|
| Total 2012 Cash Price | $4,320,000 | | | | | | | | |
| Interest Rate | 6% | | | | | | | | |
| Term (months) | 60 | | | | | | | | |
| Amortization (months) | 120 | | | | | | | | |
| | | | | | | | | | |
| | 2012 | 2013 | 2014 | 2015 | 2016 | 2017 | 2018 | 2019 | 2020 |
| Estimatd Maintable EBIT-DA (as projected) | $870,519 | $904,112 | $938,862 | $974,808 | $1,011,987 | $1,062,586 | $1,094,464 | $1,127,298 | $1,161,117 |
| Deduct Interest Charges (current) | | | | | | | | | |
| Deduct Interest Charges (proposed) | $250,354 | $230,298 | $209,204 | $186,398 | $162,397 | $136,916 | $109,864 | $81,143 | $50,650 |
| Pre-Tax Debt Adjusted Earnings | $620,165 | $673,814 | $729,658 | $788,410 | $849,590 | $925,670 | $984,600 | $1,046,155 | $1,110,467 |
| Less Income Tax | | | | | | | | | |
| Small Business Rate @ 15.5% | | | | | | | | | |
| For First $500,000 | -$77,500 | -$77,500 | -$77,500 | -$77,500 | -$77,500 | -$77,500 | -$77,500 | -$77,500 | -$77,500 |
| Prescribed Rate thereafter | -$32,445 | -$46,930 | -$62,008 | -$77,871 | -$94,389 | -$114,931 | -$130,842 | -$147,462 | -$164,828 |
| Total Taxes | -$109,945 | -$124,430 | -$139,508 | -$155,371 | -$171,889 | -$192,431 | -$208,342 | -$224,962 | -$242,328 |
| Net After Tax earnings | $510,220 | $549,384 | $590,150 | $633,039 | $677,701 | $733,239 | $776,258 | $821,193 | $868,141 |
| Deduct Net Sustaining CapEx | -$12,176 | -$12,419 | -$12,667 | -$12,921 | -$13,179 | -$13,443 | -$13,846 | -$14,262 | -$14,690 |
| Adjusted Discretionary Cash Flow | $498,044 | $536,965 | $577,483 | $620,118 | $664,522 | $719,796 | $762,412 | $806,931 | $853,451 |
| Deduct Principal Due | $325,176 | $345,232 | $366,326 | $389,132 | $413,133 | $438,614 | $465,666 | $494,387 | $524,880 |
| Net Cash Flow | $172,868 | $191,733 | $211,157 | $230,986 | $251,389 | $281,182 | $296,746 | $312,544 | $328,571 |
| Cumulative Cash Flow | $172,868 | $364,602 | $575,759 | $806,745 | $1,058,134 | $1,339,316 | $1,636,062 | $1,948,606 | $2,277,177 |

# ACCOUNTANT

Choosing the right accountant should be more than just someone who is a friend of a friend. You may want to, and also be quite comfortable with keeping your own books. I know many independent pharmacy owners who do just that. Finding the right accounting professional can make a real difference in your success. Ideally an accountant is someone who you will want to rely on to do much more for your business than its taxes or preparing financial statements. For small and medium-size pharmacy businesses or start-ups, the qualified accountant is also your consultant and business advisor.

When choosing an accountant to act as a trusted business advisor, it is crucial that you consider the following:

Not every small business requires the full menu of services offered by a particular accounting firm. Most small businesses are not too complicated and can be served by a small or smaller accounting firm, while other pharmacy businesses have more complex needs, such as group benefit plans, where they need a greater range of services from an accounting firm. You want to do your best to match your needs with the accounting firm's offering.

## INSIDE KNOWLEDGE

Accounting practices cover a broad area and not every professional is going to know the intricacies of the pharmacy industry. Do not be afraid to ask and ensure that the firm you choose has other independent pharmacy clients.

Ask the right questions to properly interview a potential accountant or firm. Here are some basic questions, courtesy of an experienced accounting colleague of mine.

- Will I be assigned the same accountant each time or multiple accountants?

- Who can I call if I have a question?

- What are your normal business hours?

Fees matter obviously, but it is not the only consideration. It is important to clarify up front the scope of services you are looking for and actually need. Do you need a bookkeeper, tax preparer or full-scale business consultant? Different professionals will offer different levels of service.

Accountants will typically be involved in their professions as members of associations and other professional groups. Many of these require continuing professional education, ensuring members stay on top of the latest accounting and tax changes. Make sure the accounting firm you choose is connected and up to date.

There needs to be a level of personal comfort in addition to professional confidence in your accountant or accounting firm. As a trusted advisor you need to know and be comfortable with the accounting professional you are relying on (personal chemistry). Do not be afraid to check references.

Staying connected and communicating when financial issues come up is very important. You want an accountant who will pick up the phone, return a text, or answer email in a timely manner. In today's world of multiple communication devices, it is important to clarify up-front the means by which pharmacy owner and accountant will be talking. No one method will be better than another, but both parties will have to be on the same page in order for the relationship to work.

Review your annual financial statements together. Find out in advance when to expect the financial statements to be ready for personal review after your year-end is complete. In a start-up, you will also want to ask if you can rely on your accounting professional to provide short-term financials (i.e. 1st quarter results). This will give you the added ability to track progress based on your business plan/Pro forma.

## VALUATION CONSULTANT

Know what your potential acquisition is worth. Many pharmacy owners have no idea what their pharmacy business is worth today, and if they think they know, they are probably wrong. Some independent pharmacy owners have a sentimental view of their pharmacy's worth which often gets in the way of good judgment. For a potential acquisition, it is important to be able to establish a valuation in a timely manner. Remember that there may be as many as 50+ interested buyers, buying groups or corporate acquisitions teams looking at the same potential acquisition.

Learn the financial condition of the potential acquisition. Some pharmacy owners may think they understand the financial health and value of their company; however, having an independent third party valuation analysis including tangible and intangible assets can confirm or deny the selling price proposed by the pharmacy owner or their representative.

I have spoken to many independent pharmacy owners who have heard of another independent pharmacy not too far away selling for a significant amount. The statement then soon follows that "My pharmacy must be worth that much as well as we have similarly sized pharmacies". Unfortunately this is not always the case. There are specific "key performance indicators" (KPIs) which can come into play, which may see two pharmacies relatively close in a specific trading area be valued differently.

Knowing a valuation consultant who is familiar with the intricacies and nuances of independent pharmacy can be invaluable in achieving your ownership goals if you are choosing to be a pharmacy owner through an acquisition.

# CHAPTER FOUR –
# PLANNING

## PLANNING AN ACQUISITION

When you are planning an acquisition, you may have had the thought or been approached by another colleague who is also interested in ownership and would like to form a partnership. Either way, the most important step towards forming a partnership is to establish a shareholder/partnership agreement. This agreement is essential and needs to be properly drafted by a mutually agreed upon and qualified lawyer as a legal agreement between the partners prior to making an acquisition.

You may think that prior friendship with your partner or partners will be enough to have a foundation for a solid working relationship, however, in my experience that is rarely the case. Typically friendship based partnerships work for a short time; however, when issues arise over the sharing of expenses and profits or when the business has grown to a significant size, the onset of disputes is guaranteed.

Several years ago I had contact from a young partnership that had been started by two bright, young pharmacy professionals that had completed a start-up. At a point in their first year of operations, one of the partners showed up one day with a pharmacy technology devise that cost several thousand dollars. His partner asked why he had bought it, and his partner told him that they were going to need it if they were going to explore a new facet of professional service they had discussed weeks before. Not only was his partner upset by the sizeable expense without his prior knowledge, but he was also upset because the discussion surrounding the new facet of professional service was incomplete.

Through further inquiries in my discussions with the partner who had called me for advice, I discovered that not only did they not have a shareholder/partnership agreement in place, they did not have a written business plan prior to their pharmacy start-up.

Shareholder/partnership agreements need to clearly define such things as how expenses will be handled and, for example, how large an expense needs to be in dollars before it needs the approval of all the partners/shareholders. The shareholder/partnership agreement should also cover how profits will be divided and what types of shares various partners will hold. For instance, will partners active in the day-to-day operations of the pharmacy business hold different shares than partners/shareholders who are not involved in the day-to-day operations of the pharmacy?

The thing to remember is shares have five rights:

1. Voting rights          or    no voting rights;
2. Dividend rights        or    no dividend rights;
3. Redemption rights      or    no redemption rights;
4. Retraction rights      or    no retraction rights;
5. Right to equity value  or    no right to equity value.

Good solid legal council is essential to establish the shares that should be issued initially for a pharmacy business. Most lawyers that I have spoken to over the years advise to keep the share structure simple initially. Whether the shares issued are common or preferred, you may not know what rights should be associated until later on in the life of the pharmacy company. Partnerships are the quickest way to engineer a business and can make a sizeable difference in the success of the pharmacy. What is most important is the shareholder/partnership agreement. The following are some basic considerations for a partnership.

## DIVISION OF PROFITS AND EXPENSES

You and your partners could have different ideas about how profits and expenses should be divided up and distributed and each of you will certainly have different financial goals. It is important that you determine from the onset whether profits will be allocated in proportion to a partner's percentage interest in the business. When will the partners be able to withdraw profits from the pharmacy company? For example, will each partner be entitled to a regular draw of the profits from the business, or will he or she have to wait for the profits to be distributed at the end of each fiscal year end?

## BUSINESS DECISION-MAKING

How do you allocate responsibility for decision-making? Over the course of a business day an independent pharmacy owner has to make hundreds of decisions. You should discuss the various types of decisions, such as operational, staffing, financial, customer service, etc., a pharmacy owner needs to make, and establish decision-making procedures for the daily pharmacy business operations. There is no standardized guide for success. In one circumstance you may require a unanimous vote by all the partners. In other cases you may decide that based on the circumstances and cost amount, (minor expense) the partner confronted with the decision can make it on their own. Your partnership/shareholder agreement will have to describe what is classified as a major or minor decision.

## TAKING ON NEW PARTNERS

Eventually you may want to expand the business and bring in a new partner or partners, or perhaps look to make a second acquisition or start-up. Agreeing on a procedure in advance for admitting new partners will make your lives a lot easier when this issue comes up. Now would be the right time to speak with your lawyer as partners and decide if the current share structure and rights are sufficient for taking on more partners. Perhaps the new partner will be one which is only interested from an investment position, and he or she will not be involved in the day-to-day decisions of the pharmacy business.

## PROVISION FOR THE DEATH OF A PARTNER

Equally important as the rules for admitting new partners to the business are the rules for handling the untimely death of a shareholder/partner. It does happen. You should decide as partners in your shareholder/partnership agreement how the shares will be handled at the time of death of one of the partners. What if the deceased partner's shares are now legally held by the deceased partner's spouse? Will the spouse be able to hold the shares or will those shares be handled differently? Will the spouse be able to sell those shares to an outside third party? Good legal counsel in the structure of a shareholder/partnership agreement can make these extremely difficult circumstances much clearer.

## PARTNER SUCCESSION

What happens if for reasons of retirement or lifestyle change, a partner wants to sell their shares and move on? Who will get those shares if there are two remaining partners? Will the shares be divided equally among the remaining shareholders? How will those shares be valued? Does the shareholder/partnership agreement have a "right of first refusal" provision which states that if a partner wishes to succeed from ownership in the pharmacy business, their shares must be offered to the remaining shareholders and cannot be offered to an outside third party? Will the partner who is succeeding from ownership in the pharmacy business be required to sign a "non-compete" which will define their ability to open a new pharmacy or work for another pharmacy.

## SHOT GUN CLAUSE

As a quick overview, the shot gun clause provides that one shareholder may make an offer to buy the other shareholder's interest (shares) at a price set by the shareholder making the offer. That being said, what makes this clause appropriate for some partnerships, is that by having made the offer to buy, that shareholder has also now considered to have offered to sell their interest at the same price and on the same terms as the offer to buy. Now it is left up to the shareholder receiving the offer to decide whether or not they want to sell their interest, or whether they want to purchase the interest of the other shareholder.

The shareholder initiating the offer must think through the process and the price offered for the shares. If they make a lower than current fair market value offer, they may end up being bought out at that low price. This clause needs to be discussed in detail by all partners with good legal advice to decide whether or not the shot gun clause is suitable.

## STAGED BUY-OUTS

A staged buy-out can be a good strategy for making an independent pharmacy acquisition. It means making an acquisition over a period of time (5-7 years) by purchasing shares initially and at predetermined points over the agreed upon period of time. Many independent pharmacy owners that I have spoken to have a key issue that needs to be addressed in order for them to establish a succession plan which would consider a staged buy-out, in particular, "Legacy".

Independent pharmacy owners looking to succeed from ownership will consider a staged buy-out as a hedge against the disappearance of the legacy that their pharmacy represents in the community. They are only comfortable in selling if the new owner understands the successes and legacy represented by the pharmacy business over many years. To ensure that the legacy goes forward, an independent pharmacy owner will take on a junior partner, typically with some experience and a skill set that suits the current business plan. Once again the business plan in question is not written, but is an oral history, which can be determined through dialogue with the existing owner.

If you are presented with an opportunity to own an independent pharmacy through a staged buy-out, then you must remember that similar principles still apply as previously discussed. The main step is to establish a shareholder/partnership agreement which states how many shares you can purchase as your initial buy-in. What is the value of the shares for the initial buy-in? In addition, the shareholder/partnership will have to include the points discussed above and in particular, when further shares will be available for purchase (i.e. on each anniversary date of the initial buy-in), and how those shares will be valued in the future.

An important point to make here is that after your initial buy-in you find that your impact on the business has seen significant growth in the pharmacy business, which ends up being reflected in the value of the business and obviously the shares. In short, your hard work ends up costing you more in the future purchase of shares as prescribed by the shareholder/partnership agreement. One can also argue that if this is the case, then the profits will increase as well as a result of your hard work and impact on the pharmacy business.

Staged buy-outs as a strategy for independent pharmacy ownership are becoming more common, however, they need to be understood and require a sensitive touch to succeed. Many common staged buy-outs happen as a result of a staff pharmacist or pharmacists (techs as well) of an independent pharmacy, who approach the owner with the idea of a staged buy-out when the owner wishes to gradually step away. Owners will typically be excited about the idea as the staff is intimate with the current business plan and legacy as well as the current client base and day-to-day operations. The sensitive touch here is that negotiations can get sensitive and should never be part of the work place environment. A third party M&A consultant should be hired to negotiate and mediate the process in able to protect the day-to-day business from inappropriate distractions.

## AFFILIATION

Another key decision to make, whether doing a start-up pharmacy or making an acquisition, is whether or not you want to belong to a banner group, a franchise or perhaps a buying group.

## BANNER GROUPS

There are numerous banner groups in the Canadian retail independent pharmacy marketplace. These banner groups have been very successful in helping independent pharmacy owners with a collective identity and marketing strategy that is applicable in just about any geographic region in the country. The success of these banner groups is based on the collective strength and buying power of older members across the country. As a result, these buying groups will have compliance driven components of their banner agreements which gives them performance and negotiating power with vendors.

One of the key compliance components of the banner group is typically a formulary for prescription drug purchases. The prescription drug formulary is pre-determined and the members are expected to comply to receive the maximum benefit available through the banner group's negotiations with specific vendors.

Each banner group has a business plan based on their years of experience and success in the Canadian retail pharmacy marketplace. Some independent pharmacy owners, who are not affiliated with the banner group, argue that the reason they remain unaffiliated is that the compliance driven components of the banner group take away their true independence in business making decisions. Independent pharmacy owners who belong to banner groups argue that the compliance driven components of the banner group program provides strength and comfort knowing that the banner group is taking care of these issues collectively and helps manage their pharmacy businesses effectively.

Another mandatory component of most, if not all banner groups in the Canadian independent pharmacy marketplace, is the existence of a ROFR or right of first refusal agreement. Right of first refusal agreements will vary from banner group to banner group. However, regardless of individual terms and terminology, they basically mean that when an owner who belongs to the banner group decides to sell their pharmacy, they must present any offers to the banner group, which has the right to exercise the right of first refusal on any offers presented. As mentioned previously, some independent pharmacy owners see the right of first refusal agreement as taking away from their independence. However, owners of banner group pharmacies will see the right of first refusal as a way of perpetuating the banner group for the foreseeable future.

So how do you decide whether a banner group is right for your start-up or for an acquisition? I think it comes down to this: if you take the time to write a business plan that reflects your business goals and you take time to understand the business plan of the banner group you are in dialogue with, then it is a simple choice of whether your business plan and the banner group's business plan have compatibility. It is important to ask the right questions before you join the banner and to clearly understand the documents you are going to sign if you decide to join the banner group. This can make a huge difference in your relationship with the banner group now and in the future.

# FRANCHISES

The structure of a pharmacy franchise can be somewhat different than that of a banner group. Ownership in a pharmacy franchise is typically different than ownership in a banner group. For example, an owner of a banner group pharmacy will have their name on the master lease throughout its term, whereas the pharmacy franchisee may not have their name on the master lease at all.

Typically the investment required to become a pharmacy franchisee is not as significant as becoming a banner group pharmacy. In essence you are partnering with the franchise which gives you the advantage of less financial exposure at start-up. Many young pharmacy professionals see this as an advantage. However, in my conversations with pharmacy franchisees, many of them feel that the franchise agreement and its compliance based components do not give them the independence they desire, whereas other pharmacy franchisees feel that the franchise program gives them strength, marketplace identity, and less stress in terms of day-to-day operations.

I think the same process is important if you are considering a pharmacy franchise. Make sure that your business plan and the franchise's business plan are compatible and that you clearly understand the terms and conditions of the franchise agreement before you sign. I would also strongly recommend that you have a lawyer review the documents and discuss them prior to signing.

# BUYING GROUPS

Many independent pharmacy owners in Canada decide not to become affiliated with a banner group or franchise and create their own branded identity in the community. Many of the non-affiliated pharmacy owners join buying groups. Most of the buying groups are affiliated with wholesale distributors of pharmaceutical pharmacy related products.

What many of these independent pharmacy owners like about buying groups is that there are less compliance driven components of the buying group agreements, and typically no right of first refusal agreements if they choose to sell their pharmacy at any point in the future. As a result, independent pharmacy owners who belong to these buying groups are obligated to make more of the decisions on what products and services they provide. Many pharmacy owners see this as an advantage because it allows them to adapt their product and service offerings to accommodate new business plans and to quickly make changes to react to the marketplace and competition.

# PHARMACEUTICAL WHOLESALERS

So you might ask – where do pharmaceutical wholesalers fit in, in terms of banner groups, pharmacy franchises, and buying groups? All banner groups and pharmacy franchises will have service contracts with various pharmaceutical wholesalers. Buying groups are offered typically through pharmaceutical wholesalers, and as a result, using a pharmaceutical wholesaler that markets the buying group is mandatory for buying groups.

Banner groups and pharmacy franchises have negotiated service contracts which include the terms from the pharmaceutical wholesale under contract. On the other hand, buying group members may have more flexibility and negotiating terms with the pharmaceutical wholesaler marketing the buying group.

# PROCESS

## NEGOTIATIONS

You can't just enter into negotiations and say "Here's my price". At the very least, you'll have to justify that figure on the basis of sound reasoning and an accepted methodology. This isn't the time to look unprofessional or unprepared with a lot of wishful thinking or ridiculous demands. Contrary to some thinking out there, the independent pharmacy marketplace is not full of idiots who are willing to let you "make a killing" at their expense. I have seen some other potential buyers think they can bully their way to a conclusive deal on a pharmacy acquisition.

A well-prepared presentation is your best ammunition for negotiating a fair price for a pharmacy business, including respect towards *the engagement process* as discussed above and the seller's wishes in terms of their *comfort zone*. Any time you enter into negotiations you can expect that the other side has done some form of valuation as well, and you can also expect that their work has produced a figure that may be vastly different from yours.

Price is always a compromise between what the seller's want (sometimes a highly subjective amount) and what the pharmacy is actually worth to the buyer. It is totally legitimate to say that the same pharmacy is worth different amounts to different buyers or buying groups simply because one might be able to do more with it than another. For instance, a particular buyer might have another pharmacy that would integrate well with their company. Combining the two would result in certain advantages, such as building an ownership portfolio, "brand" or market share. Whatever the particular advantages are, the pharmacy will be worth more to this buyer than to someone else, so there's a good chance that they, or their company, will be willing to pay more for it.

Acquiring a good independent pharmacy is full of challenges and a lot of competition. Being prepared to get engaged in the race is going to allow you the best chance of success. Clearly understanding the preparation, planning and process of a potential acquisition is essential.

## THE ACQUISITION PROCESS

Many younger pharmacy professions that I speak with commonly think that if they have some cash assets, with access to credit, that they are ready to make an acquisition. This also holds true for the established owners group who wish to use the equity they have built in their current ownership portfolio to make further acquisitions.

What is equally important is a keen understanding of the acquisition process. In my experience when a good pharmacy is available for sale, I can easily bring through my network, 75–100 interested individuals or buying groups/teams, but only those who have a clear understanding of the acquisition process will be engaged to a point of potential success. There are a high percentage of potential buyers who never get close to a potential acquisition because they do not understand the acquisition process and inevitably lose out because the opportunity is gone before they get a chance to sit at the table and discuss it in more detail. Let's break the acquisition process down based on the following:

- Signing a non-disclosure agreement;

- Initial due diligence;

- Letter of intent;

- Further due diligence;

- Closing.

As discussed earlier, the first step is knowing that your cast of supporting professionals are ready and aware of your hunt for the right pharmacy acquisition. Your cast of supporting professionals need to know your progress and timeline to enable them to act on your behalf in a timely manner.

## SIGNING A NON-DISCLOSURE AGREEMENT

The next step is that you *should* be required to sign a *non-disclosure agreement* (NDA). The **NDA** that you should be signing will unpack the terms and conditions regarding the sharing of proprietary information for the potential acquisition. It is important for the pharmacy owner to establish how and under what terms the proprietary information is shared and for how long. In addition, the NDA will determine how that information may be transmitted and with whom it can be shared for the purposes of performing due diligence. The NDA should explain what is proprietary and what might be determined as common industry knowledge. It is also advisable to have your lawyer review the NDA before signing.

## INITIAL DUE DILIGENCE

The initial due diligence should occur once you have received the proprietary documents for the potential acquisition. The documents in question should be, but are not limited to the following:

1. 2-3 years of third party prepared financial statements (P&L, Balance Sheet, Statement of Owners/Shareholders Equity).

2. 2-3 years of matching Rx summary reports inclusive of corresponding Rx gross profit dollars, dispensing fees, mark-ups and any rebates.

3. A copy of the current lease including square footage, gross and selling space, annual basic rent, other occupancy fees and common area and maintenance costs (CAM), remaining term on lease, renewal terms, and special lease terms or restrictions.

Upon receipt of the above information, you and your professional group of advisors should begin the initial due diligence as soon as possible. Any initial questions for clarity on the information noted above should be asked and confirmed as well.

The next and most essential step is to establish a valuation for the potential acquisition and determine if the pharmacy owner's asking price is reasonable or worth potential negotiations. Some independent pharmacy owners will not provide an asking price and will take offers instead. In either case, arriving at a value is essential to move forward and decide whether or not you wish to pursue this opportunity.

## LETTER OF INTENT

The letter of intent or LOI is the next step towards a potential acquisition. Some buyers use LOI templates or have their lawyer draft one up. If you choose an LOI template, I would recommend you have your lawyer review the LOI before presenting it. The LOI will typically lay out the terms and conditions of the proposed acquisition, as well as the price, closing date and conditions precedent, as well as other considerations. The price and closing date tend to be negotiable, however, the "conditions precedent" refers to the items to which the potential buyer must be satisfied or completed before he or she can move forward towards closing.

In the majority of cases the pharmacy owner prefers a "non-binding" LOI and so should the potential buyer. The simple reason is that a non-binding letter of intent allows either party to step away from the potential deal at any point prior to closing if conditions precedents are not met, or if either party has a change of mind. You may think this is wasting the time of both parties; however, it is a cost effective way of moving forward to determine if the buyer and seller are a good match and if it works for both sides. An example of non-binding language in a letter of intent may look like the following.

> "Other than the covenants contained in paragraphs ___ of this Letter of Intent, this LOI is not binding upon either the Purchaser or the Seller, and is subject to the negotiation and execution of a definitive share (or asset) purchase agreement between the parties."

There is typically some binding language and it usually surrounds the "confidential information exchanged" as well as "terms of the negotiation", to name a few, to protect the buyer from the seller shopping the offer. All letters of intent will state that the potential new owner reserves the right to keep or not keep any of the current employees, and that if they decide not to keep any of the current staff members, any severance and or holiday pay is the responsibility of the seller. Buyers need this provision, sellers hate it. However, in the majority of cases, the staff remains intact with few exceptions, as the staff does tend to represent a portion of goodwill, and it is to the buyer's advantage to initially keep them.

# FURTHER DUE DILIGENCE

The "conditions precedent" in the letter of intent lay the foundation for further due diligence and they can be made up of a few of the following more common requests:

1. The ability to speak with the landlord and discuss the lease and typically the possibility of an extension based on where the owner is currently in the term.

2. The ability to seek and confirm financing based on the final negotiated price as described in the letter of intent.

3. To interview and determine whether all the staff will remain under the new ownership.

4. Determine the relationships with the doctors.

5. Determine basic operational standards.

6. Review contracts with long-term care or other facilities where service is provided by the pharmacy.

Further due diligence is usually the first time the potential buyer gets to meet the seller and visit the pharmacy (after hours). The further due diligence process needs to be discrete to keep the knowledge of the negotiations away from the pharmacy staff and customers. The worst, and I mean the worst thing a potential buyer can do, is walk into a pharmacy and say to the owner or staff, "I heard your pharmacy is for sale?" This usually ends any further dialogue.

# CLOSING

Once the NDA has been signed and the initial due diligence is complete, the non-binding letter of intent has been presented, negotiated and signed, and further due diligence is satisfied, and everyone is still smiling at each other, then it's time for the lawyers to take over. Usually the buyer's lawyer will initiate a draft version of the purchase agreement to the seller's lawyer based on the terms of the letter of intent. The document will typically go back and forth a few times for clarity and once complete, and both parties are content, the purchase agreement is ready for signing at the agreed upon closing.

# CHAPTER FIVE –
# PREPARATION (START-UP)

The preparation for a start-up pharmacy includes the same steps as outlined earlier in this book. The difference between a start-up independent pharmacy and an acquisition is that now you have to apply your business plan to the start-up as a blueprint. When making an independent pharmacy acquisition, you inherit the owner's business plan, and have to find a way to blend your plan into the existing plan. With a start-up pharmacy, your business plan and Pro forma come into play from day one.

## COMMERCIAL REALTOR

If you are looking for the right location for a start-up pharmacy, you need to consider the value of your time. Having a list of properties available and their advantages with respect to your pharmacy business's best market location can seem overwhelming. Commercial realtors can bring experience and a solid understanding of the available commercial space in your area and can help sift through the locations which are not ideal for your pharmacy business, thus saving you considerable time. Getting in your car and driving through an area which appeals to you in terms of a potential location for your start-up is impractical.

In addition to avoiding the heavy investment of time just to find the right location, additional time savings can be realized as the desired location progresses, in organizing inspections, negotiating and re-negotiating terms, and completing paper-work. The commercial realtor has experience and connections to search for a location as well as the ability to streamline the completion of all the necessary steps to signing the lease.

There is also a con to the time element of using a commercial realtor. Your agent does not get paid until the deal is signed. This may motivate him or her to rush the process along without giving full consideration to your pharmacy business needs. You will need to be aware of this fact in order to insist on moving the process along at the speed that is best for your phar-macy business.

Commercial realtors' market knowledge can provide an edge. They pride themselves on knowing the local market and can help individual pharmacy ventures find the most potentially profitable spots for their pharmacy business.

Commercial realtors often know quickly which spaces are available and most suitable for your pharmacy business, plus any restrictions, zoning, and proposed development the indi-vidual might not be aware of. They are familiar with areas, trends, and local business owners and landlords, all of which can provide an edge to the individual in their search for the right independent pharmacy space. They also invest capital in proprietary reports on market data as well as traffic counts, demographics, and comparable leases and sales.

Successful lease negotiations can be stressful. A commer-cial realtor negotiates for a living and can provide a buffer between the sometimes difficult process and the individual client. Negotiations can be complex and it is helpful to have an advocate on your side that can advise you each step of the way before you sign the lease.

Leases are legal documents which no one likes to read. They are confusing and full of legal expression that can often be difficult to understand. A good commercial realtor can read and interpret these legal documents and help negotiate lease clauses that could be potentially harmful to the individual client.

Finding the right location for a pharmacy start-up includes the closest proximity to the offices of general practitioners (GPs). Having a location near other healthcare professionals can be advantageous as well, however, as you know the potential working relationship with general practitioners is essential to the success of the pharmacy. Make sure to have the assistance of the commercial realtor in finding the ideal location for your independent pharmacy start-up. Take time to share key components of your business plan with him or her to help them understand your goals and specifics of the location required for success before choosing.

# PLANNING A START-UP PHARMACY

## WORKING THE BUSINESS PLAN

Now that you have completed the business plan and have shared it with your cast of supporting professionals, it becomes your blueprint for your start-up pharmacy. At this time you will be in regular contact with your commercial real estate agent. Based on your business plan, they will be actively seeking the right location for your start-up pharmacy. Your business plan will also clearly define the approximate square footage for your start-up pharmacy. In addition, you have also discussed with your commercial real estate agent the importance of having your location in close proximity to doctors' offices or clinics where there are general practitioners.

Some start-up pharmacy owners look to include square footage for a walk-in clinic. Including a walk-in clinic is currently a trend for existing independent pharmacy owners as well as start-up pharmacies. This trending model of presenting a pharmacy with a medical clinic attached or as part of the general retail space is to provide patients with convenience and access to a broader healthcare environment in one location. I will be speaking about this trend later on in the book.

Part of the business plan for a start-up pharmacy is the costs associated with starting or building a pharmacy from scratch. Many first-time pharmacy owners that have decided to do a pharmacy start-up are not really aware of the many costs associated with leasing and building out a pharmacy space. Included in the start-up costs are numerous licenses and permits required to build out an approved new pharmacy start-up.

## START-UP (GREENFIELD) COSTS

If you have decided to do a start-up pharmacy, where do you begin? Included below, is a spreadsheet provided by a colleague of mine, Guy Shaddock. Guy is an experienced professional pharmacy designer. This spreadsheet was developed to list possible pharmacy start-up costs. The items on the list show you how many considerations there are and the cost implications associated with each step and category.

**Sample Costs for a 1200 sq ft Pharmacy**

| Design & Tenant Improvements | Estimate | Rev Estimate | Comments | Actual | |
|---|---|---|---|---|---|
| Design/Project Management Fees | $6,500 | | | | |
| Permits | 400 | | | | |
| Demo Washroom to make accessible | 400 | | This may be a landlord cost | | |
| Cut Slab for Elec chases | 300 | | Feeds for islands | | |
| Rough carpentry | 1,500 | | This is a "plug"...a guess | | |
| Doors and Hardware | 1,400 | | Doors 103 104 105 106 107 108  Based on $200/door.  Landlord costs? | | |
| Drywall | 2,500 | | This is a plug | | |
| Ceiling 2x4 Tbar $2/sq ft | 2400 | | Based on $2/sq ft x 1200 sq ft | | |
| Painting | 3,000 | | This is a plug | | |
| Flooring supply/install Marmorette $7/ft | 8,400 | | Based on $7/sq ft x 1200 sq ft | | |
| Window Coverings | 0 | | | | |
| Electrical | 11,000 | | Includes 41 Lights @ $200/light | | |
| Data and Telephone | 1,200 | | Terminations and set up | | |
| Music and Speakers | 500 | | | | |
| Plumbing HC Wash + 2 Sinks | 3,500 | | Move lavatory and add two sinks | | |
| Clean up | 400 | | Bin and labour | | |
| HVAC | 3500 | | Distribution (this is a plug) | | |
| Sub-Total | $46,900 | | Sub of above | | |
| General contracting (20%) | 9,380 | | Calculates 20% on Subtotal above | | |
| Millwork and Fixtures | 44,000 | | May be reduced if Vic drug bays are reused in the Compounding Room | | |
| Contingency | 4,690 | | 10% of all Tenant Improvement costs | | |
| Total | $104,970 | | | | |

| Signage Furniture Equipment | Estimate | | | Actual | |
|---|---|---|---|---|---|
| Vinyl Graphics to windows | 1500 | | | | |
| Interior signage * | 500 | | | | |
| Exterior signage * | 5,000 | | | | |
| Computer/printer(s) software/training/setup | 10,000 | | | | |
| Library | 0 | | | | |
| Dispensing Equipment | 0 | | | | |
| Phone Lines installed and equipment | 1000 | | | | |
| Chairs @ $90 each 4-8 chairs | 360 | | | | |
| TV | 0 | | | | |
| VCR | 0 | | | | |
| Fridge | 250 | | | | |
| Vacuum | 150 | | | | |
| Fax machine | 250 | | | | |
| Safe | 250 | | | | |
| Office Supplies | 750 | | | | |
| Security system install | 1,200 | | | | |
| Total | $21,210 | | | | |

| Marketing Supplies | Estimate | | | Actual | |
|---|---|---|---|---|---|
| Print package (stationery) | $1,500 | | | | |
| Marketing materials | | | | | |
| Medical visual library | | | | | |
| Rx labels & labeler | | | | | |
| Rubber stamps | | | | | |
| Total | $1,500 | | | | |

| Professional Fees & Training | Estimate | | | Actual | |
|---|---|---|---|---|---|
| Business License | 125 | | This is a plug | | |
| Legal and accounting | $1,000 | | This is a plug | | |
| Wholesaler Shareholder fees | $15,000 | | | | |
| Pharmacist license fees - initial | 1,200 | | | | |
| Total | $17,325 | | | | |

| Pre & Grand Opening Costs | Estimate | | | Actual | |
|---|---|---|---|---|---|
| Advertising flyers – printing & distribution, ads * | $5,000 | | | | |
| Promotional product * | | | | | |
| Temporary help | | | | | |
| Screenings | | | | | |
| Total | $5,000 | | Rev Estimate | | |

| Inventory | Estimate | | | Actual | |
|---|---|---|---|---|---|
| Rx | $60,000 | | | | |
| OTC | 30,000 | | | | |
| Total | $90,000 | | | | |

## Summary

| | | | |
|---|---|---|---|
| Design & Tenant Improvements | $104,970 | | Indicates value with quote on file |
| Signage Furniture Equipment | $21,210 | | |
| Marketing Supplies | $1,500 | | Indicates a cell with a calculation |
| Professional Fees & Training | $17,325 | | |
| Pre & Grand Opening Costs | $5,000 | | Do not imput data calculation cells |
| Inventory | $90,000 | | |

*Plug means a guess

Total of all Categories   **$240,005**

## Sample Costs for a 1200 sq ft Pharmacy

| Design & Tenant Improvements | Estimate | Rev Estimate | Comments | Actual | |
|---|---|---|---|---|---|
| Design/Project Management Fees | $6,500 | | | | |
| Permits | 400 | | | | |
| Demo Washroom to make accessible | 400 | | This may be a landlord cost | | |
| Cut Slab for Elec chases | 300 | | Feeds for islands | | |
| Rough carpentry | 1,500 | | This is a "plug"... a guess | | |
| Doors and Hardware | 1,400 | | Doors 103 104 105 106 107 108  Based on $200/door.  Landlord costs? | | |
| Drywall | 2,500 | | This is a plug | | |
| Ceiling 2x4 Tbar $2/sq ft | 2400 | | Based on $2/sq ft x 1200 sq ft | | |
| Painting | 3,000 | | This is a plug | | |
| Flooring supply/install Marmorette $7/ft | 8,400 | | Based on $7/sq ft x 1200 sq ft | | |
| Window Coverings | 0 | | | | |
| Electrical | 11,000 | | Includes 41 Lights @ $200/light | | |
| Data and Telephone | 1,200 | | Terminations and set up | | |
| Music and Speakers | 500 | | | | |
| Plumbing HC Wash + 2 Sinks | 3,500 | | Move lavatory and add two sinks | | |
| Clean up | 400 | | Bin and labour | | |
| HVAC | 3500 | | Distribution (this is a plug) | | |
| Sub-Total | $46,900 | | Sub of above | | |
| General contracting (20%) | 9,380 | | Calculates 20% on Subtotal above | | |
| Millwork and Fixtures | 44,000 | | May be reduced if Vic drug bays are reused in the Compounding Room | | |
| Contingency | 4,690 | | 10% of all Tenant Improvement costs | | |
| Total | $104,970 | | | | |

| Signage Furniture Equipment | Estimate | | | Actual | |
|---|---|---|---|---|---|
| Vinyl Graphics to windows | 1500 | | | | |
| Interior signage * | 500 | | | | |
| Exterior signage * | 5,000 | | | | |
| Computer/printer(s) software/training/setup | 10,000 | | | | |
| Library | 0 | | | | |
| Dispensing Equipment | 0 | | | | |
| Phone Lines installed and equipment | 1000 | | | | |
| Chairs @$90 each 4-8 chairs | 360 | | | | |
| TV | 0 | | | | |
| VCR | 0 | | | | |
| Fridge | 250 | | | | |
| Vacuum | 150 | | | | |
| Fax machine | 250 | | | | |
| Safe | 250 | | | | |
| Office Supplies | 750 | | | | |
| Security system install | 1,200 | | | | |
| Total | $21,210 | | | | |

| Marketing Supplies | Estimate | | | Actual | |
|---|---|---|---|---|---|
| Print package (stationery) | $1,500 | | | | |
| Marketing materials | | | | | |
| Medical visual library | | | | | |
| Rx labels & labeler | | | | | |
| Rubber stamps | | | | | |
| Total | $1,500 | | | | |

| Professional Fees & Training | Estimate | | | Actual | |
|---|---|---|---|---|---|
| Business License | 125 | | This is a plug | | |
| Legal and accounting | $1,000 | | This is a plug | | |
| Wholesaler Shareholder fees | $15,000 | | | | |
| Pharmacist license fees - initial | 1,200 | | | | |
| Total | $17,325 | | | | |

Sample Costs for a 1200 sq ft Pharmacy

| Pre & Grand Opening Costs | Estimate | | | Actual | |
|---|---|---|---|---|---|
| Advertising flyers – printing & distribution, ads * | $5,000 | | | | |
| Promotional product * | | | | | |
| Temporary help | | | | | |
| Screenings | | | | | |
| Total | $5,000 | | | Rev Estimate | |

| Inventory | Estimate | | | Actual | |
|---|---|---|---|---|---|
| Rx | $60,000 | | | | |
| OTC | 30,000 | | | | |
| | | | | | |
| Total | $90,000 | | | | |

### Summary

| | |
|---|---|
| Design & Tenant Improvements | $104,970 |
| Signage Furniture Equipment | $21,210 |
| Marketing Supplies | $1,500 |
| Professional Fees & Training | $17,325 |
| Pre & Grand Opening Costs | $5,000 |
| Inventory | $90,000 |

Total of all Categories **$240,005**

Indicates value with quote on file

Indicates a cell with a calculation

Do not imput data calculation cells

*Plug means a guess

Please note that the costs represented in this start-up spreadsheet are provided as examples only. There are many variables especially where construction is concerned. Nevertheless, it is helpful to establish an initial bottom line and it helps you to start thinking about a **budget**. In this case the total costs of all categories are based on averages for a pharmacy that is 1,000 – 1,100 square feet. It is important to consult a pharmacy design expert who will have a clear understanding of your business plan, location and budget, etc.

In addition to establishing start-up costs described above, you will need to fill out an "Application for New Pharmacy" form from your Provincial College of Pharmacy. Page 1 from the BC College of Pharmacy looks like the following:

# APPLICATION FOR NEW PHARMACY

## Community

## APPLICANT INFORMATION

☐ Corporation

☐ Sole proprietor / Partnership

Cert. of Incorporation # _____     Incorporation Date _____

Company name _____

Address _____     Tel _____

_____     Fax _____

_____     Email _____

_Postal code_

| Director * | Pharmacist | Director * | Pharmacist |
|---|---|---|---|
| _____ | ☐ | _____ | ☐ |
| _____ | ☐ | _____ | ☐ |

* Majority must be BC registered pharmacists

## PROPOSED PHARMACY INFORMATION

Operating name _____

Address _____     Tel _____

_____     Fax _____

_____     Manager _____

_Postal code_

Contact + _____

Opening date _____     Tel + _____

Software Vendor _____     Fax + _____

+ Only if manager not available before opening

## PAYMENT OPTION

☐ Cheque/Money order _(payable to College of Pharmacists of BC)_

☐ VISA     ☐ MasterCard

Card # _____     Exp ____ / ____

Cardholder name _____

Cardholder signature _____

| | |
|---|---|
| Initial Licence Fee | 1,331.00 |
| GST | 66.55 |
| **Total** | **$1,397.55** |

GST # R106953920

I attest that:

☐ The Pharmacy is in compliance with the Health Professions Act, the Pharmacy Operations and Drug Scheduling Act, the Pharmacists Regulation and the Bylaws of the College of Pharmacists of British Columbia made pursuant to these Acts.

☐ I have read and understood the Pharmacy Licensure in British Columbia – Information Guide and Resources package.

☐ I will maintain a valid business licence for the duration of the pharmacy licence.

_____     _____
Name (please print)     Signature

_____     _____
Position     Date

College of Pharmacists of British Columbia | 200 - 1765 West 8th Ave Vancouver, BC, V6J 5C6 | Tel: 604.733.2440 | Fax: 604.733.2493 | www.bcpharmacists.org

Applications must be received by the College office at least 10 weeks prior to the proposed opening date. It is a good idea to discuss this application form with your pharmacy design consultant to ensure compliance based on your provincial college application forms compliance specifications and time frame.

# THE LEASE

The lease is a very important document and you will benefit by knowing how leases work before you are in a position to sign it. Once signed it is extremely difficult to make changes. In addition, it is a major expense and being in control (understanding wise) of your lease will work in your favour. You should always have a trusted advisor, such as a lawyer, commercial realtor etc., review your lease or lease renewal prior to signing. Here are some considerations for signing or renewing a lease. Allow enough time for a start-up lease agreement and get started nine months ahead of time to avoid unexpected situations and delays.

Lease renewal negotiations should begin 12 months before the term expires. This will give you enough time to look at other sites and do your due diligence. If you cannot get a decent renewal rate, would you rather find out you need to move with three weeks or six months left on your lease term? Time will be on your side or your enemy depending on how you use it.

Establish your bargaining strength. Several indicators will determine your bargaining strength in regards to negotiating a new lease or renewal. These include the overall vacancy rate of the building and recent tenant turnover. Your unit's size in relation to the entire property is also relevant. It is not only whether you occupy 1,000 or 5,000 square feet, but also what percentage of the building you occupy.

## LEASE RENEWAL ALLOWANCES
Pharmacy business owners often don't think they can negotiate for a tenant allowance on their renewal term. Most only think

they can negotiate tenant improvement allowances (TIs) at the initial signing of the first lease. That is not the case. Remember, if the landlord is giving allowances to new tenants moving in, then why can't you get a renewal allowance as well?

## WHEN SHOULD THE LEASE END?

Most independent pharmacy owners try to launch their start-up pharmacy going into the busy season (which makes sense). However, most lease terms should generally expire at the end of a peak season or just going into the company's slow period. It is usually better to negotiate a shopping centre tenant's renewal in February rather than October. Therefore, rather than taking a five-year (60-month) term, opt for a 56 or 64 month term. Start and end your term when it's best for you, not just the landlord.

## KEEP YOUR SUCCESS CONFIDENTIAL

One of the main reasons a tenant will be forced into a rental rate increase for a renewal term is the landlord's belief that the tenant can afford to pay it. The better your pharmacy business is doing, the quieter you must be about your success. It is important to instruct your staff regarding how successful the pharmacy is as they are often the ones who may speak directly to the property manager.

## REQUESTS FOR PROPOSALS MUST BE WRITTEN

When negotiating a new lease or renewal, it is most desirable that the landlord or property manager's proposal be in writing. A landlord might not automatically send you a renewal proposal at the end of your term. If your calls go unanswered, send the landlord a letter requesting a renewal proposal within 10 days.

## ANTICIPATE YOUR LEASE ASSIGNMENT

Landlords anticipate that you will eventually sell your business and that you will want to assign your lease agreement—you should too. We have seen some lease agreements that say that the landlord can unilaterally terminate a tenant's lease rather than grant an assignment. On the other hand, landlords can automatically raise the rent for the new tenant (the buyer). Check this clause carefully before you agree to it, then negotiate for changes.

## CASH BURN

Cash burn is defined as: The rate at which a new company uses up its cash resources or capital before producing a positive cash flow. The burn rate is usually expressed as the amount of capital used per month.

Cash burn is an important measure for how a start-up pharmacy company will perform and how it should be properly capitalized. I have spoken to many pharmacy professionals who are working on a business plan but have not included a Pro forma. The Pro forma will indicate the amount of cash burn projected forward from start-up to a point where the pharmacy breaks even and begins to show a profit. This information is essential when presenting your business plan/Pro forma to a bank or other lending institution.

Remember, the lender may not really understand the points of your business plan that express the scope of practise you are planning to offer your customers as well as the supporting services or products. They do, however, need to see how that professional practise business plan translates into cash and how much cash flow would need to be generated to sustain the business (break-even point).

# CHAPTER SIX –
# PROCESS

## SIGNING DOCUMENTS

Make sure before you sign any documents, whether the document is a lease, a letter of intent, the purchase agreement, a service contract, banner group agreement, franchise agreement, or buying group agreement, that you seek good legal counsel and understand clearly the implications of what you are signing before you sign.

## OWNERSHIP LIFESTYLE

### COUNTING THE COST

When you work for an employer you know your annual salary and perhaps there is little opportunity available to earn more money on your job. Starting or acquiring your own pharmacy business gives you the potential to earn a higher salary. Your business plan is completely under your control and the income you earn relates to the activities and success of your business plan. Although earning a higher salary is not a guarantee, the potential to earn a much higher income is very possible.

Owning or starting a pharmacy business gives you the opportunity to work in a profession and industry that you have trained for and that you can enjoy. Working in a profession you are passionate about helps you better handle peaks and valleys in your business. Owning your own business allows you to be creative and contribute your energy, which gives you personal satisfaction. Most pharmacy professionals working in the industry they enjoy also bring their experience and expertise, which allows them to offer innovative products and services and a new scope of practise to customers.

Owning or starting your pharmacy business gives you the control over your business. Some individuals thrive in situations where they experience independence. Owning or starting a pharmacy business gives you the power to control how active you are in the business. You can participate in every step of the decision-making process or you can hire or form partnerships with competent people to help make decisions in the best interest of the company.

Many independent pharmacy owners work long and erratic hours, and some people view this as a disadvantage. Work schedules are the most gruelling for new pharmacy owners because they usually handle time-consuming administrative tasks. The responsibility of running the business ultimately rests upon your shoulders. You may experience days when you need to stay in the office until the task is complete or until you find the time to do it.

A disadvantage of owning or starting a pharmacy business is that you must incur financial risk. Whether you used your own savings or borrowed money for start-up costs or for making an acquisition, the money invested in your company is at risk. Some pharmacies go out of business and cause the owners to lose their initial investment or default on business loans. Even with a solid business plan, economic or industry volatility can cause your pharmacy business to lose money and eventually close for good.

Depending on your business structure, creditors and vendors may possess the ability to seek your personal assets if you default on your business obligations. If a vendor believes you acted in error, he may file a lawsuit against you. To protect your company's assets, you can seek liability insurance for your business, but some new business owners may find it difficult to afford insurance premiums.

It's a good thing to take time and think through your business plan and seek good council from your cast of supporting professionals as well as industry experts at the beginning of your preparation for independent pharmacy ownership to ensure your best chance of seeing positive results. Whether your pharmacy is a start-up or a first pharmacy acquisition, make sure you *count the cost of ownership.*

# "IF YOU BUILD IT, THEY MAY NOT COME"

## BUILT-IN CLINIC/OFFICES

There seems to be a growing number of pharmacy professionals who wish to renovate and divide their existing pharmacy or do a start-up pharmacy to include a doctor's office/walk-in clinic. This holds true for both the established owners group and the younger pharmacy professionals.

A few months ago I spoke with a younger pharmacy professional who wanted to do a start-up pharmacy, and when I spoke to him he had already signed a lease. I asked him if he had written a business plan. He told me he had a plan, however, it was not in written format. His plan included building in a walk-in clinic for general practitioners. He did not know the allocation of space between the retail pharmacy and the walk-in clinic. In addition, when I questioned him further, I asked him if he understood the cost of building the clinic portion of his pharmacy. He did not understand that the millwork costs alone would significantly increase as a result of building in a walk-in clinic. He was under the impression that if he provided space and facilities for general practitioners, that it would be a simple task to attract doctors. Because he had already signed a lease and had not been consulted on the cost of building in a walk-in clinic, his current ability to capitalize his start-up based on the financing was greatly diminished.

As you may know there is currently a shortage of general practitioners. As a result, many mature general practitioners are unable to sell their practices simply because a new general practitioner who has recently graduated from medical school can easily open up a location and have as many patients as they desire. Because of this retail pharmacy trend, many corporate and independent pharmacy owners are offering general practitioners little or no rent to move into facilities specifically designed for them, which are currently part of the retail pharmacy space.

I spoke recently to another pharmacy owner. We will call him Ryan. Ryan is a mature pharmacy owner whom I have worked with in developing a succession plan. Once complete, Ryan was ready for me to market his pharmacy for sale on his behalf. Just as I was getting ready to market Ryan's pharmacy, Ryan decided he was going to subdivide the existing retail pharmacy space to include a walk-in clinic. The cost to do so was significant, and by doing so, Ryan thought it would be easy to attract general practitioners by offering free rent as well as a turn-key walk-in clinic. Ryan was disappointed and frustrated at how difficult it was to attract general practitioners who are now being approached regularly to move into retail pharmacy locations providing space for walk-in clinics.

## DOCTORS AGREEMENTS
Don't get me wrong, I think building a pharmacy business plan, whether existing or new, to include a walk-in clinic for general practitioners is worthwhile. The problem I see is that the plan

to include a walk-in clinic in a retail pharmacy location is not thought through thoroughly. The walk-in clinic/pharmacy model business plan should be written in detail and include the costs of building out a retail space to include both. In addition, the business plan should indicate visa vie the Pro forma, the monthly cost of the subsidy that the pharmacy business will absorb to host the walk-in clinic.

Equally important as including the details of this in your business plan, is to also have an agreement between you and any potential general practitioners you attract to join you in this retail space. In speaking to a number of general practitioners regarding being approached to move into a walk-in clinic/pharmacy model, the consensus was that the majority of general practitioners do not believe that anything is truly free. As a result, many general practitioners are reluctant to dialogue further with independent pharmacy owners who approach them regarding a walk-in clinic/pharmacy model.

What I have recommended to a number of my clients who are interested in establishing a walk-in clinic/pharmacy model, is that they produce a **License Agreement** before they approach any general practitioners. Since independent pharmacy owners are not sub-letting the space for the walk-in clinic to the general practitioners or including them on the master lease, a license agreement is appropriate to establish the parameters of the relationship going forward.

This license agreement needs to include the terms and conditions of the relationship between the pharmacy owner and the general practitioners occupying the walk-in clinic, including covenants to establish what is actually free and what is not. In other words, a pharmacy owner may offer general practitioners who occupied the walk-in clinic free rent and utilities, however, that does not include the cost of a receptionist, or perhaps computers, or other medical clinic related equipment, software, lab coats, etc. The license agreement should also include the term as well as potential termination of the relationship between the pharmacy owner and the general practitioners occupying the walk-in clinic.

Another valuable covenant is assignment of the agreement, so that if the independent pharmacy owner decides that he or she wishes to sell their pharmacy, inclusive of the space occupied by the walk-in clinic, that the license agreement is re-assignable. I strongly recommend that if you are considering building a walk-in clinic/pharmacy model, that you provide a license agreement before you approach any general practitioners to join you.

It is essential therefore, to sit with your lawyer and discuss this walk-in clinic/pharmacy model in detail, to assist your lawyer in helping you draft up a proper license agreement, and to get proper legal advice before you enter into a formal agreement with general practitioners who are interested in occupying the space provided in the walk-in clinic.

# CHAPTER SEVEN –
# SELLING AN INDEPENDENT PHARMACY (PREPARATION)

*"Whether it's letting a company go, a responsibility, a job, or accountability, perhaps even a friend – it's not easy!"*

## WHERE'S THE PLACE TO BEGIN TO THINK ABOUT SELLING?

Let's look at where the statistics are in terms of owner-ship succession.

A recent Canadian Federation of Independent Business (CFIB) research document produced the most current succes-sion statistics from a 2011 survey on small to medium enter-prises (SMEs) in Canada (which is inclusive of all independent pharmacies). Some key points from this sizeable document suggest the following issues.

# TRANSITION/SUCCESSION

The most common method among SME owners of exiting their businesses is to sell outright to non-family members (37%). This is surprising given the large presence of family businesses in the economy. One in four (26%) business owners indicated that they intend to sell or transfer their business to a family member in the future, while a similar share does not currently have plans.

# THE SUCCESSION PLAN

*Only one third (35%) of SMEs have a plan to sell, transfer, or wind down their business in the future. However, among those with a succession plan, it more likely to be unwritten and informal as opposed to one that is formal.*

## SUCCESSION PLAN DEVELOPMENT

The development of a succession plan often requires the input and services of various professionals such as accountants and legal advisors, internal stakeholders in the business such as key managers and employees, as well as family members and the successor(s), if already chosen. The most common types of professional assistance used in developing a succession plan are accountants and lawyers. Use of other professional services is significantly lower.

## THE SUCCESSOR

Among SME owners who have already chosen a successor for their business, the majority resort to a member of the family. A family member currently working in the business tends to be the most popular choice (58%), with family not employed in the business accounting for only 6%. In contrast, the most likely choice for a successor among business owners who have not yet chosen a successor is someone from outside the family, such as an employee, competitor or supplier.

## NO SUCCESSION PLAN

Among those business owners who do not have a succession plan, the majority (60%) indicated that it is too early to plan. However, professional advisors indicate that it is never too early to start planning. The lack of adequate time to plan and execute succession is a significant contributor to failed successions. There is a significant perception that succession can occur over a relatively short period of time.

## SUCCESSION BARRIERS

Most barriers identified by professional advisors are, as previously mentioned, commonly considered "soft" in nature. Such is the case when the owner avoids dealing with succession due to their strong personal sense of attachment with the business. In other instances succession is difficult due to conflict with family members or key employees. Technical barriers include legal, financial, and legislative restrictions to planning or executing a succession. The CFIB survey sought to identify both soft and technical barriers faced by current SMEs who are planning their succession, as well as those who recently took over a business through succession. However, the single largest barrier to succession can be identified by those who do not have a succession plan altogether.

## BARRIERS FOR CURRENT OWNERS

According to current owners, the number one barrier to succession planning and execution is the financing of their successors (46%). Finding a suitable lender or buyer comes in a close second with 42% of owners citing it as a barrier.

Those businesses with at least one family member employed, however, are less likely to cite finding a successor as a barrier relative to those who do not employ family (35% vs. 58% respectively). Among the "soft" issues, 39% of owners indicated that the dependence of the business on their active involvement is an obstacle to succession. Although owners are often advised to seek professional assistance, 12% identified the availability of cost-effective planning and professional advice as a barrier.

This gap between service providers and business owners may be a primary cause to other barriers, which include the formal valuation of the business (32%). The valuation of the business can also result from the dependence on the business owner's involvement which accounts for "goodwill".

Conflict among family members was ranked relatively low as a barrier and differs significantly in family and non-family run businesses. Among family businesses, 17% of the owners cited conflict with family members; however, the business owners indicated that the family members are performing extremely well on a number of fronts.

Since undergoing a succession, over half of successors surveyed increased the total employment of the business, and only 11% decreased employment. Moreover, the majority of these businesses have experienced increased profits (68%), increased market share (60%), and a greater number of product and services offered to customers (67%).

Clearly there are significant economic benefits of successful transitions beyond the maintenance of current employment and output. Successors are bringing new entrepreneurial vigour to existing businesses and with it greater opportunities for employees, their communities, and the economy.

> **"Succession planning is not just about what you leave behind ... It's also about what lies ahead."**

> *"You built this pharmacy. You watched it grow. You invested sweat equity and money in it. When you decide to exit, why wouldn't you expect your business to give you something back?"*

Early succession planning enables you to:
- Maximize the value of the business and its potential selling price;
- Explore a broader range of succession and ownership transition options;

- Take the time to choose the right team of advisors and acquaint them with the pharmacy business;

- Set up the proper financial goals; and

- Have a positive impact on your business's long-term viability/legacy.

## SUCCESSION OVERVIEW

Let's look at the basic structure of a succession plan. A good working succession plan does not have to be 30 pages long. What is important is that the structure of the succession plan is inclusive of some key discussion points.

1. Desired outcome and legacy:

Typically when I meet and discuss formulating a succession plan with an independent pharmacy owner, the conversation quickly comes to a point where money is the focus of the discussion. After discussing a few of the points listed below the conversation shifts towards another major discussion point which is legacy. A good succession plan addresses both the financial return of selling an independent pharmacy as well as the legacy that the pharmacy business represents in the community.

   a. Staying on with part ownership (staged buyout);

   b. Staying on during ownership transition (three months to one year);

   c. Clean break, no desire to stay involved post-closing;

   d. Name change;

   e. Affiliation change;

   f. Staff changes by new owner;

   g. Pharmacy location closed/files moved.

2. Supporting cast of professionals:

The list below of the supporting cast of professionals has been discussed earlier in the book, however, when developing a succession plan it is important to understand how essential it is to have these professionals involved in the decision-making process.

    a.  Mergers and Acquisitions Consultant (M&A Consultant);

    b.  Valuation analysis (What is my pharmacy worth?);

    c.  Accounting professional (tax advice - shares or assets);

    d.  Financial planning (retirement or investing post-closing proceeds).

## OTHER INDUSTRY CONSULTANTS

I want to take more time here to discuss how essential it is to work with an M&A Consultant to assist you with a succession plan as well as work on your behalf to reach the best possible outcome.

When you have established a succession plan for your pharmacy business, you have two choices on how to market your pharmacy for sale. You can try to sell it yourself by using a "for sale by owner" approach, or you can engage an M&A Consultant to represent you in selling the pharmacy business. An M&A Consultant is a professional intermediary who helps pharmacy owners find potential buyers for their pharmacy business and helps the owner negotiate the terms of the sale for the best possible outcome. There is no requirement for a pharmacy owner to engage an M&A Consultant to sell a pharmacy business. The M&A Consultant will charge a fee for the services provided and the fee is largely commission based.

By choosing a "for sale by owner" approach, a pharmacy owner will avoid paying a commission, and many pharmacy owners see this as an advantage not to engage an M&A

Consultant. That being said, those pharmacy owners fail to consider the cost of going the "for sale by owner route;" in particular, the cost of potentially leaving money on the table.

I continue to run into circumstances where independent pharmacy owners engage real estate agents to represent them in the sale of their pharmacy. I am also contacted regularly by real estate agents who represent independent pharmacy owners who are trying to sell their pharmacies. It is clear to me that real estate agents don't know where to begin in terms of marketing an independent pharmacy for sale. Real estate agents in question consistently call me and ask for my assistance to help with their clients' succession needs. I have not seen the skill set and goals of real estate agents and their knowledge of the pharmacy industry align with the goals of the independent pharmacy owner.

In my experience, as an M&A Consultant for independent pharmacy owners, the efforts and added cost of the M&A Consultant, in many cases, will return to the business owner much more than the commission paid. This is because the interests of the M&A Consultant are in sync with the interests of the pharmacy owner. The higher the price, the more each will receive when the transaction completes which is a "win, win" situation. In other words, an owner who uses an M&A Consultant can end up with more money than an owner that does not, even when the commission is taken into consideration.

Selling a pharmacy business is a skill in and of itself which is different from the skill of running a business. Even though most pharmacy owners are highly skilled at running their businesses, they are not skilled at selling their business. These are two entirely different skill sets and experimenting in selling without fully understanding how to do it can have serious negative consequences. I know of pharmacy owners who have sold their pharmacies on their own that have made serious mistakes primarily because they don't know what is "normal" in the sale of a pharmacy business. An M&A Consultant works on numerous transactions, and knows what sale terms are reasonable and what are unreasonable. This expertise can save a pharmacy owner tens of thousands of dollars, easily covering the commission charged.

Most pharmacy owners have worked very hard on their business and have built up valuable equity over a long period of time. That being said, buyers want to pay as little as possible for the pharmacy business, so in an effort to get the lowest price, the buyer will tend to point out all the negatives of your pharmacy business including operational issues, inventory, number of staff members, to name a few. This inevitably will insult the pharmacy owner and be seen as an attack on the owner and his pharmacy. Emotions will then start to come into play and a pharmacy owner attempting a "for sale by owner approach" would be very vulnerable. The pharmacy owner will be offended and will refuse to continue to negotiate. The deal then typically falls through or the pharmacy owner gets worn down by the buyer and ends up agreeing to a bad deal out of frustration.

Using an M&A Consultant allows the pharmacy owner to take a step back and keep their emotions away from the deal. The end result is a better deal gets structured and can move towards completion. In my experience, as an M&A Consultant, I usually deal with many potential buyers with many different acquisition strategies.

If the pharmacy owner goes it alone, what typically can happen is a potential buyer will approach the pharmacy owner directly, and work slowly to get to know the owner on a personal or a somewhat professional level. When the timing is right, the buyer makes a "verbal offer" to purchase the business. At the same time, the buyer will try to convince the pharmacy owner not to talk to any other potential buyers. This may be exciting to the pharmacy owner; however, it typically results in the business owner getting a price lower than current fair market value. To get the best price it's best to engage as many interested and qualified buyers. In my case, via my website Rxownership.ca, I am contacted by buyers regularly seeking good pharmacy acquisitions.

M&A Consultants know where most of the buyers are. They will look objectively at your business, tell you what you need to do in order to get the best possible outcome, and will then go to work marketing the pharmacy to as many potential and qualified buyers as possible.

There are also other value-added benefits to pharmacy owners in using the services of an M&A Consultant. Much of the work you would otherwise have to do to sell your pharmacy will be done for you. For example, the M&A Consultant will put together the marketing documentation that buyers will not expect to see. This documentation is called a CIM (pronounced 'sim') which stands for Confidential Information Memorandum. The CIM becomes a valuable marketing document which contains all the foundational information a buyer would want to know in order begin their due diligence in order to make a decision to investigate the purchase further. A pharmacy owner, with a "for sale by owner" approach and acting without an M&A Consultant, will be unsure how much information to provide to potential purchasers. The result is often the release of propri-etary information when not required or in a worst case scenario, proprietary information given to potential buyers without a non-disclosure agreement signed beforehand.

The M&A Consultant will work with you to ensure the right amount of information is released to keep interested and quali-fied buyers engaged. In the meantime, the pharmacy owner can stay focused on running the business.

An M&A Consultant also plays another role very effectively. In the sale of a pharmacy business some challenging issues can arise. It can be time consuming and expensive to have your lawyer and the potential buyer's lawyer arguing about these issues. On the other hand, an M&A Consultant can take on the role of mediator, in effect looking at the problem from both sides. This will result in a resolution being reached faster, the transaction being more likely to complete, and the seller getting the best possible outcome. Having an M&A Consultant play this role can save the business owner money and make it more likely that a deal will close.

# CHAPTER EIGHT –
# THREE TYPES OF BUYERS

My experience as a Mergers and Acquisitions Consultant has brought me to the conclusion that there are three main groups of buyers active in the independent pharmacy marketplace.

## MANAGEMENT BUYERS

Staff or pharmacy managers who wish to be in ownership will be typically looking for the owner to carry part of the financing. Many independent pharmacy owners have been approached at some point by a pharmacy staff member who has shown interest in perhaps one day purchasing the pharmacy business. The advantage of this is that the pharmacy staff member in question has an intimate understanding of the day-to-day operations, legacy, customers, etc. Many pharmacy owners see this as an advantage.

The disadvantage of this type of proposal is not just that the staff member may want the owner to carry some of the financing, but also any discussions and negotiations can get personal and cause adverse effects between the owner and the staff member. It's good to include a Mergers and Acquisitions

Consultant if you wish to choose a staged buy-out as your succession plan.

# FINANCIAL BUYERS

These are first time buyers with appropriate financing as well as independent pharmacy owners wishing to expand their pharmacy ownership portfolio, typically by leveraging equity in existing pharmacies. Other financial buyers are owners of an existing pharmacy who are now willing to take on partners and are looking to expand their ownership portfolio through acquisition. In most cases, the financial buyers are individuals who own multiple pharmacies, and are looking to expand their established brand through acquisition.

# STRATEGIC BUYERS

Corporate entities, who have experienced, well-equipped and knowledgeable acquisitions teams, are actively seeking acquisitions. Most independent pharmacy owners I speak to, have at one point or another been approached by members of these corporate acquisitions teams. Sometimes the contact is made in person and other times through correspondence sent directly to the pharmacy. The challenge of being contacted directly and in person by a member of one of the corporate acquisitions teams is that it is very difficult to discuss any aspect of ownership transition within earshot of staff and customers. Corporate acquisitions teams are very knowledgeable when it comes to valuations. However, it is difficult to discuss the value of your pharmacy over a cup of coffee or lunch if you have no idea what your pharmacy is worth, or if you really don't know how the acquisitions process works.

These buyers are looking more at the metrics of an acquisition based on their corporate marketing strategies and agendas.

They will also introduce "Earnout Provisions" in some acquisitions. Earnout Provisions will be discussed in more detail later.

The three points mentioned above are a good foundation for
a jumping off point to begin structuring a succession plan. Each
of these points at some stage represent secondary discussions
that should take place between you, your cast of supporting
professionals, colleagues and other trusted industry consultants.

# CHAPTER NINE – THE CORPORATE RECORD BOOK

Existing pharmacy companies and start-up pharmacy businesses might view keeping corporate records as a low priority. Large companies usually have their lawyers keep their minute books up to date, but that can be expensive for smaller pharmacy companies who may not have a lawyer or law firm that they engage for smaller tasks. In my many discussions with lawyers I have compiled what items should be kept in your minute book and why it is important to stay current with corporate records.

In general, your pharmacy company's minute book should have records for all formal board of director and shareholder actions and resolutions, as well as a complete record of share ownership. In addition, your company's minute book should include a copy of the articles of incorporation and bylaws as well as any amendments to these documents.

You might be wondering why you should keep current with your minute book or even have one at all. Below are a few of the important reasons to keep a minute book for your company.

The minute book leaves a trail that enables owners and lawyers to look back at the decisions and transactions of a corporation. The minute book is an important audit backup. The minute book can help determine effective dates for tax purposes and establish justification for the accrual of operating expenses and other obligations.

Up to date records can help you avoid challenges to the corporation's authority to take certain actions. These challenges might come from minority shareholders, fellow directors, employees or government agencies. Your corporate minutes are important records of the authority granted to the corporate officers and directors to act on behalf of your pharmacy company.

The minute book establishes the background record needed by your lawyer to support certain legal opinions. When a corporation undertakes a certain transaction, it is often necessary to obtain a legal opinion regarding the corporation's history as well as current authority for such a transaction. An example may be something as simple as securing financing from a bank or other lending institution.

The corporation's minute book should include shareholder records. This section needs to be carefully kept current because it is the one true ownership record of the shares in the corporation. Ownership is not officially recorded anywhere else. Your minute book should reflect exactly when and to whom shares of the pharmacy company have been transferred. It is sometimes a good idea to keep the original stock certificates of the owners with the minute book – this prevents the certificates from becoming lost and prevents shareholders from selling their stock without the corporation's knowledge.

Your minute book is extremely important if you ever decide to sell your pharmacy company. Any potential buyer is going to want to look at your minute book to ensure all actions have been properly taken. This will help the potential buyer evaluate any outstanding liability your company has. For example, if your pharmacy company merged with another pharmacy company in the past, but you do not have the records showing a board resolution approving the merger, a potential buyer might ask to decrease the purchase price based on this outstanding liability.

If you can't remember the last time you updated your minutes, now is a good time to give your lawyer a call. If you are just starting a company, you should contact an attorney to help you set up a minute book.

## HISTORICAL RECORDS

Minutes serve to provide a historical record of the important transactions which have taken place during the life of a corporation, including major purchases, sales of assets, loans, and leases to name a few. Other matters such as established salaries and bonuses for shareholders, key employees, contributions to company retirement plans, as well as corporate dealings with its own shareholders and directors (including loans to or from shareholders and directors) should be documented and approved as part of the corporate record. Doing so is not simply a matter of good practice; it can also serve to head off challenges brought by minority shareholders and provide support, in the event of a CRA audit, for those actions that were taken.

## OFFICER AND DIRECTOR LIABILITY

Maintaining an updated corporate minute book can help an officer or director support the fact that they have conducted themselves properly and carried out their duties and responsibilities to the corporation. This can help keep clarity and partnerships on track.

## THIRD PARTY REVIEW

Banks and lenders frequently ask to review a corporation's minute book or perhaps just the articles of incorporation, bylaws and the most recent meeting minutes or consent resolutions of the corporation.

## HARD TO RECONSTRUCT

The failure to keep an updated minute book can be problematic when attempting to reconstruct at a later date what actually happened in any given year. Annually updating the minute book serves to avoid disputes among shareholders, directors and officers as to what happened, when it happened and why it happened, which is often the case when trying to document something that took place at various points in the past.

## RESOLUTIONS

Resolutions are defined by the board of directors or members of a limited liability company. They may include things like share structure and assignments and actions voted and accepted by the board of directors.

## MEETING MINUTES

Meeting minutes are usually written and signed by the secretary of the corporation and are kept in the meeting minute's book. They should list all old and new business issues passed by the board of directors or tabled by the board for discussion as well as an agenda.

## ANNUAL MEETING MINUTES

A limited liability company is required to have at least one shareholder meeting each year. Other corporations may have more than one meeting per year. These minutes should include who is elected to the board of directors each year and a copy should be kept with your corporate records.

## COMMUNICATIONS TO SHAREHOLDERS

A copy of every communication that is made to the shareholders, whether it is via email, snail mail or facsimile, should be kept in your corporate record book.

## LIST OF SHAREHOLDERS

Keep a list of current shareholders up to date. If shareholders change, keep a record of old shareholders and how shares were transferred.

## ANNUAL REPORTS

Limited liability companies usually have to file annual reports with the province, but check with the provincial registrar to make sure.

## FINANCIALS

Year-end financials and tax returns should be kept with your corporate records as each shareholder is required by law to have access to these records. Keeping accurate and timely financials and tax returns in one place is also convenient for collecting documents when applying for additional financing.

# CHAPTER TEN –
## VALUATION

*To become aware of the key performance indicators that account for worth.*

*To determine the value of shares for a potential buy-out of a partner. Agreeing on the methodology ahead of time can present a much better outcome.*

*For estate planning and structure.*

*To be able to justify your asking price and feel confident as you move towards any offers presented.*

## SHARES VS. ASSETS

In the sale of a pharmacy business, the question whether to sell the shares of the operating company or the assets of the business is always a key discussion point. Tim Nichols, a colleague of mine who is an experienced mergers and acquisitions lawyer and a principal of Hungerford Tomyn Lawrenson and Nichols in

Vancouver (www.htln.com) puts the question of shares versus assets this way:

"This is always a central threshold question to be addressed by the parties. Every transaction is different, but in many instances the seller will prefer to sell the shares of his company, whereas the purchaser would rather acquire assets. The parties' accountants are usually involved in this decision.

These are some of the factors to be considered:

1. The tax cost to be absorbed by the seller based on each structure. If the selling company is a "qualifying small business" as defined in the Income Tax Act, some of the capital gain triggered by a sale of shares will be exempt from tax.

2. A sale of shares entails a more thorough pre-sale investigation by the purchaser because it inherits all liabilities of the business.

3. The purchaser may want to choose the business assets to be purchased. Similarly the seller may want to retain certain assets in the company. It may be necessary to transfer the retained assets out of the operating company before selling its shares. This can give rise to pre-closing tax liabilities.

4. A sale of assets is more likely to trigger a requirement for the consent of other contracting parties such as landlords.

5. Liability for GST and PST must be determined on a sale of assets. The tax will be based on how the purchase price is allocated to the assets. In most cases GST can be avoided by a joint election.

6. The treatment of existing employees of the business and all related obligations must be taken into account.

7. A sale of shares which constitutes a change of control of a company gives rise to a deemed fiscal

year end, requiring financial statements and a tax return to be prepared and filed. The sale agreement should deal with these obligations."

# EMPLOYEES

Another area of contention is the state of the seller's employees during ownership transition. This is a key point of discussion between the seller and their lawyer as part of the shares verses assets consideration. Tim goes on to explain:

"The treatment of employees of the business and related obligations in a business sale is often controversial. Depending on their length of employment, age, level of responsibility and other factors, employees may be entitled to significant severance on termination of their employment. This obligation does not appear in financial statements. A purchaser may wish to retain or rehire the employees, but must then recognize that a successor employer may be liable for the severance which has accrued before the closing date. In an asset sale, the agreement will often provide that the seller must terminate the employment of the workers on closing, with the purchaser offering them immediate re-employment on the same terms. This process is designed to crystallize the employees' severance entitlement without triggering an immediate obligation to pay. In addition to claims for damages at common law for wrongful dismissal, employees are entitled to assert claims pursuant the Employment Standards Act of BC." (To view Tim Nicols complete "Checklist of Legal Issues", please register at rxownership.ca.

# EARN-OUT PROVISIONS

As mentioned earlier, earn-out provisions are more typically used by corporate acquisitions teams, however some independent buyers and buying groups also work with earn-out provisions with certain acquisitions. I think it is worthwhile to take a longer look at what an earn-out provision is. After speaking with numerous colleagues who are lawyers, I have been able to gather the following description.

An earn-out provision is a mechanism used in a pharmacy transaction where a portion of the purchase price (typically goodwill) is withheld, and is calculated based on the future performance of the acquired pharmacy over a specified time period, post-closing. Earn-outs are intended to bridge a valuation gap between an optimistic seller and a buyer, who feels their pharmacy business is dynamic. Earn-outs allow sellers potentially to achieve a higher sale price, and provide buyers with additional comfort as they will be able to gauge the performance of their acquisition over a pre-determined period of time, post-closing. The use of earn-out is becoming more common in the current independent pharmacy climate.

An earn-out can also serve as a form of incentive-based compensation to the seller(s) continuing on as management post-closing, and will allow buyers to retain and motivate the seller (now manager) with aligned interests of maximizing performance. An earn-out used for these purposes, it might be argued, can help facilitate a smooth transition of the acquired pharmacy to the buyer, even though the seller (now manager) may no longer have the traditional role in the acquired business.

Although no standard earn-out model exists, there are several principal considerations that should be addressed in the negotiation and drafting of an earn-out provision:

- The definition and the scope of the acquired business, the performance of which will determine whether the earn-out is achieved;

- The selection of the performance metrics;

- The selection of appropriate accounting measurements used to calculate results;

- The establishment of the earn-out period and agreeing upon the payout structure;

- Establishing the ground work of who is in control of the acquired business between the buyer and the seller during the earn-out period; and

- The level of support (if any) that the buyer will commit to give the acquired business in attempting to achieve its earn-out objectives.

## NOTIFYING SUPPLIERS, THE PROVINCIAL COLLEGE OF PHARMACY, ETC.

When an offer to purchase your pharmacy is securely on its way towards the closing date, you must remember to notify the change in ownership with the provincial college, your pharmaceutical wholesale service provider, etc. as these changes take time to complete.

# CONCLUSION

**"It's all about the desired outcome".**

In conclusion, I think it's important to talk about outcomes. In speaking to so many younger pharmacy professionals, my first impression is that the majority of them have, as mentioned in the introduction, what I call a romantic view of ownership, whether that ownership desire is through acquisition or through start-up.

The easy part is imagining yourself in your pharmacy, doors open, business flourishing and your ability to exercise your profession, etc. The hard part, and where so many younger pharmacy professionals become disillusioned with owner-ship, is with clearly understanding the preparation, planning, and process of independent pharmacy ownership. So many younger pharmacy professionals I speak to frequently tell me that they have pooled some financial resources together and they are ready to do a start-up or acquisition. Many who keep to this line of thinking and go their own way get themselves into unfavourable circumstances.

My desire in writing his book is to help articulate a clearer understanding to pharmacy professionals who wish to become owners for the first time, either through start-up or acquisition.

It takes time and effort as well as understanding to develop a solid business plan that clearly defines the outcome you desire. By doing so, even though it takes more work, you can save yourself time, money and a lot of stress by doing it the right way.

In terms of independent pharmacy owners looking to establish a succession plan and a strategy for ownership transition, my experience has shown me in numerous conversations with pharmacy owners, that the majority of them are uninformed, somewhat anxious, and would rather procrastinate. As a result many independent pharmacy owners fail to have a succession plan and do not realize the outcome they are looking for. Many of them wait until it's too late, leave money on the table, and clearly don't understand the transition process while incurring more cost. It doesn't have to be this way.

Many of the independent pharmacy owners who begin to talk about an exit strategy and succession plan have told me that their anxiety is greatly reduced by speaking to the professionals mentioned in this book, and that the outcome they are looking for becomes more real than imagined as they move through the preparation, planning and process of ownership transition.

# ABOUT THE AUTHOR

Phil Hauser is a Succession and Acquisitions Consultant and has worked with Independent Pharmacy owners for the last 8 years. Prior to his specialization in this area, Phil was involved as a Director of Business Development and a Consultant for various pharmaceutical wholesalers in Canada and the US.

As a Certified Business Broker (CBB), Phil knows that selling a pharmacy is not easy and requires good planning. Equally owning a pharmacy for the first time also requires a good business plan in an ever-changing pharmacy marketplace.

Phil also engages young pharmacy professionals looking for first time ownership and has been a guest lecturer at the Faculty of Pharmacy for 4th year students at the University of British Columbia.

Rxownership.ca is a network, which provides the resources where pharmacy professionals at various stages of ownership can find the direction and services necessary to take the next step. Whether looking to own for the first time or expanding ownership portfolios, Rxownership.ca provides practical resources, which also includes steps towards exiting independent pharmacy ownership.

Phil firmly believes that for independent pharmacy to continue to thrive in the Canadian marketplace, their needs to be a clearer understanding of the preparation, planning and process of ownership or ownership transition.

Printed in Canada